Woe to You, Me

Woe to You, Me

Would You Recognize Jesus Today?

TYLER CECIL

RESOURCE *Publications* · Eugene, Oregon

WOE TO YOU, ME
Would You Recognize Jesus Today?

Resource Publications
An Imprint of Wipf and Stock Publishers
199 W. 8th Ave., Suite 3
Eugene, OR 97401

www.wipfandstock.com

PAPERBACK ISBN: 978-1-7252-7408-2
HARDCOVER ISBN: 978-1-7252-7409-9
EBOOK ISBN: 978-1-7252-7410-5

03/18/21

This book is dedicated to those who strive to understand
the last will be first, and the first will be last.

Those who do not remember the past are condemned to repeat it.

—George Santayana

Do not deceive yourselves. If any of you think you are wise by the standards of this age, you should become "fools" so that you may become wise.

—1 Cor 3:18

True knowledge exists in knowing that you know nothing.

—Socrates

Contents

Preface

THE JOURNEY OF WRITING this book has been both difficult, humbling, and empowering. I never thought I would be an author, and I let the idea behind this book drift around my mind for a long time before I decided to start typing. A year after deciding this was something I was going to pursue, I had still not written a single word as I was overwhelmed by how to begin. For 2019, I made a resolution I believed would be much easier than writing an entire book—to have an outline by the end of the year. Once I began the outline, words flowed onto the pages as if a dam had been broken. Ideas and memories once floating in my head flooded the pages. This was a very exciting time for me as a calling I believed in began to take form.

The form in which I had originally imagined for the book differed greatly than the one presenting itself on the pages. There were many times I would have to put down writing and wait to be taught a lesson myself before I could continue. The first significant milestone reached was 10,000 words, and I sat back to read the jumbled paragraphs and ideas. I wanted to take note of what needed further exploring and what needed less exploring.

What I found left me dumbfounded—three-quarters of the pages were filled with stories of things I had overcome and wanted people to know about my life. The remaining quarter of the pages explored Jesus' life and biblical teachings.

It hit me hard. I had fallen into the cycle I set out to teach how to process through and improve upon. The self-righteousness I felt called to teach against had consumed me as I pointed to my life over Jesus'—it was completely blindsiding. The realization caught me off guard, yet it both humbled and empowered me as it allowed me to better understand the significance of this lesson.

The next day I started over, blank slate and all, and this is where the prologue you read now begins. This story is not to be about me, even though you will find I use stories from my life. This lesson is not to be about my teachings, either. This story is about a man named Jesus and the radical lessons he's taught me and continues to teach me. My prayer is this book may reveal to you the importance of Jesus' lessons and how a deeper understanding of Jesus' teachings can lead to a radical transformation in our lives and churches. I am a sinner and whatever good comes from this book only comes by the grace given to me. As you will soon learn, I identify with the Pharisees more than I do with Jesus. I blame myself for Jesus' death and suffering. For this, I seek to love him with everything I have. This realization has allowed me to see and experience Jesus in much different ways than I ever imagined.

The purpose of this book is to paint a truer image of the Pharisees than the gospels depict. I believe the gospels are God-breathed truth, but I also believe they hold bias when it comes to other sects of Judaism and those who stood against Jesus. It must be remembered these books were written by the closest friends and followers of Jesus, who had to watch him executed at the hands of the religious leaders. The other Jewish sects depicted in the gospels still held power in the years after Jesus' death; consequently the gospel writers would have done their best to persuade readers to turn away from these men and instead turn to Jesus. As such, the bias' of the gospel writers is passed on to readers today.

In order to separate bias from reality, years have been spent researching historical and scholarly literature to achieve an accurate account of who the Pharisees were and what they believed. This book holds countless facts and truths, and these will be denoted and the sources cited in footnotes on the pages where found. I encourage you to do research of your own and explore the works I have put my weight behind. However, this book is not a scholarly book.

I believe the picture of the Pharisees portrayed in this book is more encompassing and accurate than many works today. However, due to the nature of the bias found in antique Jewish literature and the relevant lack of ancient manuscripts covering the Pharisees, this book may also contain slight inaccuracies. This is a self-reflective book and not meant to be used in dissertations. However, I'm confident those negligible inaccuracies do not take away from the purpose of this book. If you believe you have concrete evidence supporting opposite viewpoints found in these pages, I will enjoy discussing them with you and building upon my principles—if warranted.

I understand I do not know everything I think I know, and I would love to deepen my knowledge.

As for this book, I pray this is not another book that merely encourages readers but fails to provide realistic steps to take in order to grow. I've read plenty of books that have left me encouraged but without practical next steps, so I will do my best to provide biblical examples as well as dive into my own personal experience to assist you as you move forward. I have been through many trials in my life, and I believe many of you will be able to relate.

I pray you remember this book as part of a distinctive turning point in your life—it certainly has been for me.

Acknowledgements

I AM GRATEFUL TO have so many close friends and family who have supported, encouraged, and challenged me over the course of writing this book. I owe a special thank you to my editor and longtime-friend, Cindy Hess, who dedicated her time to assist in this pursuit. Thank you for believing in me and for the encouragement.

Lastly, I owe much to my future wife, Brooklyn. You changed my life the moment you walked in.

Abbreviations

AD	Anno Domini, meaning "in the year of the Lord." Also same as CE, or Common Era.
AKA	Also Known As
ARM	Adjustable Rate Mortgage
BCE	Before the Common Era
CCBA	Certification of Competency in Business Analysis
CEO	Chief Executive Officer
DNA	Deoxyribonucleic Acid
FHA	Federal Housing Administration
LGBTQ	Lesbian, Gay, Bisexual, Transgender, and Queer
MBA	Master's in Business Administration
MD	Medicinae Doctor, Latin for Doctor of Medicine
OCD	Obsessive Compulsive Disorder
PE	Professional Engineer
PhD	Philosophiae Doctor, Latin for Doctor of Philosophy
USD	United States Dollar

Introduction

THE MIDDLE EASTERN SUN is halfway through its descent, thankfully taking the dry heat with it. Large crowds gather together in the immense, walled courtyards, standing shoulder to shoulder as dozens more meander-in. As Passover approaches, the commotion in Jerusalem is at its yearly peak. A city usually home to 30,000 is in the process of swelling to over 180,000 as Jews from all over trek to the religious citadel.[1] Part of the Jewish faith requires able-bodied believers to make the trek in remembrance of the great Exodus, where Moses led the Israelite slaves out of Egypt after more than 400 years of captivity.[2]

There aren't enough inns and homes in the city of Jerusalem and those who cannot afford the inflated price of hospitality build makeshift camps on the hills and valleys outside the walls of the holy city. At nighttime during Passover, the flicking fires of the camps dot the Kidron Valley and its surrounding hills resembling fireflies dancing against a starless sky. At higher vantage points, such as atop the nearby Mount of Olives, the landscape is serene as sounds from the throngs of thousands are muted.

The dry, hot winds of the Khamsin make the nights in the mountains bearable as they roll eastward from the Mediterranean, as is typical during this time in Jerusalem.[3] It's a welcome relief from the too-recently-experienced Israeli winter—springtime has finally arrived. If only life could be full of such moments as this.

As night comes, tens of thousands worn and beaten bodies sink onto ground-cooled mats, as crackling and smoldering fires lull them to sleep.

---

1. "Passover in Israel—Past and Present," Chosen People Ministries, 2020.

2. Exodus 34:23 reads, "Three times a year all your men are to appear before the Sovereign Lord, the God of Israel."

3. "Local Mediterranean Winds," Mediterranean Sailing, Cruising, Navigation.

Amid pleasant dreams, no one has any notion that the next day will bring tragedy when a local tradesman voluntarily seals his death sentence.

By late morning, the hot sun blasts money changers and merchants alike as they man their booths lined against the temple walls. The shrine, one of the most incredible construction feats of the ancient world, features massive stone walls that surround an enormous raised plateau known as the Temple Mount. On the north and south sides of the plateau resides the Court of Gentiles. The Court of Gentiles is separated by the temple itself, with the temple's walls running almost the entire length east to west across the center of the plateau. Along the outer rim of the interior of the Temple Mount's walls is a covered path where the early arrivals set up their booths for protection against the elements. The wall directly behind them allows the merchants to keep an eye out for would-be thieves.

The temple rises far above the inner walls. While everyone is welcome on the Temple Mount, only Jews are allowed to enter the temple. All others must remain outside, hence the name the Court of Gentiles. After passing through the inner walls, Jews enter a small courtyard known as the Court of Women where Jewish women mix amongst other Jews. Only Jewish men are allowed to proceed into the temple to offer the yearly sacrifice of atonement for their own sins and those of their families.

Outside the relative calm of the temple itself, thousands are hurriedly converting money to the temple currency, the shekel, and purchasing animals to sacrifice.[4] The firefly-esque backdrop from the night before recreates itself as sunlight shimmies off the dancing coins flying around the temple.

The bleating of sheep and the clucking of chickens permeates the dozens of languages and accents. Many sojourners are searching for food stalls to recuperate from the long journey. Amid the laugher, languages, merchant calls, and sounds of livestock, many find it difficult to hear their own thoughts. The sensory overload is doubled by the smell of baked fish and fresh bread that oozes through the crowd. It could be classified as chaos, but this is what is expected at this time of year and only adds to the excitement.

People from all over the Middle East and Northern Africa, as well as Southeastern Europe are catching up with each other. Pilgrims who see each other only once a year meet new babies, hear success stories, and learn of the somber passing of once-common faces.

This year there is even more to talk about—as stories of a potential prophet add to the anticipation. A man by the name of John has been

---

4. Bill O'Reilly and Martin Dugard, *Killing Jesus: A History*, Page 137.

baptizing people in the nearby Jordan River. He preaches a message of repentance and people have heard him claim he is "preparing the way for one whose sandals he is unworthy to untie."[5] Nearly all the people find this message incredibly odd, considering slaves are the only people whose status is so low that they are not worthy to untie somebody's sandals, and slaves aren't worth talking about.

Whoever he claims is coming must be remarkable, the people think.

Even more intriguing is the blatant disregard John seems to hold for Herod Antipas and his marriage to his brother's wife, Herodias.[6] The people know Herod as the Roman-designated ruler of Galilee.[7] If he enjoyed the idea of a long life, this John fellow surely didn't show it as he openly condemned one of the region's top rulers.

At the same time, John was known to have a diet consisting of only locusts and wild honey. Any man crazy enough to sustain himself on insects is clearly not a man set on living very long. And that was another curiosity . . . a man who doesn't desire to live long is preparing the way for someone.

"*Could this mean the one prophesied about for centuries may actually come?*" The rumors only continue to broaden as the festivities ramp up.

John the Baptist says someone greater is coming. He also doesn't seem to plan on living long based on his diet. And now he's openly condemning Herod Antipas. His time is coming to an end which means one thing—who is coming and when?

Those thoughts can wait, though, as religious teachers and prophets have prophecied about a coming Messiah for as long as Israel has existed.[8] At this point, the prophecies are about as interesting as the local desert's forecast: dry, hot, and no rain, again. *Surely it will be centuries before anything good happens.*

With that will also come a few more ambitious crazies with unfulfilled forecasts. As for now, anyways, the present moment brings something more intriguing than talk of a messiah.

Word is quickly spreading about a commotion in the courtyard. A group of high-ranking religious leaders stand at the center of the crowds.

---

5. John 1:27, Mark 1:7, and also Luke 3:16.

6. Matthew 14:3–4 says, "Now Herod had arrested John and bound him and put him in prison because of Herodias, his brother Philip's wife, for John had been saying to him: "It is not lawful for you to have her."

7. Bill O'Reilly and Martin Dugard, *Killing Jesus*, Page 173.

8. Examples are Zechariah, Ezekiel, Malachi, Isaiah, among others.

Standing directly across from the leaders is a band of wanderers. They are skinny, dirty, and ragged from traveling. Their battered tunics stand in stark contrast to the clean, silk-robes worn by the religious leaders. Dust and dirt and constant sweat have taken their toll on the thinly woven linen.

One of the nomads stands out from the rest. The Nazarene stands confidently in stature, seeming somehow different from his companions. His long, oily hair batts against his cheeks in the waning breeze. The dimming light highlights his leathery skin as it casts shadows across his face.

Murmurs reverberate. Many have heard the rumors about these men. Some have heard their relatives tell stories of personal encounters with the leader of this scraggly band. There are even those who've encountered him themselves, and some are secret believers of the legends and eager to see how today's scene unfolds before revealing themselves publicly.

The religious leaders facing the Nazarene are the most popular and respected men in Jewish culture. These men have spared no expense on their wardrobe. Their long blue silk robes adorned with tassels allow them to be spotted from a hundred yards away.[9] Their positions are highly regarded. They are known by almost all of the pilgrims traveling to Jerusalem because of what they've accomplished for the Jewish nation. They have created a safe way for Jews to practice their faith in plain sight of Rome, something unheard of in the brutal history of Roman imperialization. It's a miracle the Jews weren't slaughtered like the rest of Rome's conquered and this is, in part, due to diligence from these religious leaders. They come from prominent families and are well educated. As such, they've been able to convince the Romans to allow the people to live and practice their faith. They hold the power to create Jewish laws and pass judgement on people. For centuries, they have been the ones to bring people to the God of Abraham and to erase the sins of the people. A comfortable life can be found within the inner circle of these men—one of wealth, popularity, and power.

The societal barrier between the two groups couldn't be more profound.

This is the moment the crowd has hoped for. Sure, the two groups have butted heads before, but there has not been a better time to set those differences aside and band together. The future of a free Jewish Nation depends on it. The Nation and land that has been promised for centuries is closer than ever, if only the Nazarian carpenter and his followers can unite with the power and influence of the religious leaders.

9. O'Reilly and Dugard, *Killing Jesus*, Page 17.

Introduction

The Nazarene takes a step forward. The crowd waits as the lowly wanderer addresses the most powerful men in Jewish culture. Surely, they think, he has come to renounce his claim of divinity and to pledge his support to their ways. Then and only then can the Kingdom of God be established by overthrowing the Romans.

The man speaks.

13"Woe to you, teachers of the law and Pharisees, you hypocrites! You shut the door of the kingdom of heaven in people's faces. You yourselves do not enter, nor will you let those enter who are trying to. [14]

15"Woe to you, teachers of the law and Pharisees, you hypocrites! You travel over land and sea to win a single convert, and when you have succeeded, you make them twice as much a child of hell as you are.

16"Woe to you, blind guides! You say, 'If anyone swears by the temple, it means nothing; but anyone who swears by the gold of the temple is bound by that oath.' 17You blind fools! Which is greater: the gold, or the temple that makes the gold sacred? 18You also say, 'If anyone swears by the altar, it means nothing; but anyone who swears by the gift on the altar is bound by that oath.' 19You blind men! Which is greater: the gift, or the altar that makes the gift sacred? 20Therefore, anyone who swears by the altar swears by it and by everything on it. 21And anyone who swears by the temple swears by it and by the one who dwells in it. 22And anyone who swears by heaven swears by God's throne and by the one who sits on it.

23"Woe to you, teachers of the law and Pharisees, you hypocrites! You give a tenth of your spices—mint, dill and cumin. But you have neglected the more important matters of the law—justice, mercy and faithfulness. You should have practiced the latter, without neglecting the former. 24You blind guides! You strain out a gnat but swallow a camel.

25"Woe to you, teachers of the law and Pharisees, you hypocrites! You clean the outside of the cup and dish, but inside they are full of greed and self-indulgence. 26 Blind Pharisee! First clean the inside of the cup and dish, and then the outside also will be clean.

27"Woe to you, teachers of the law and Pharisees, you hypocrites! You are like whitewashed tombs, which look beautiful on the outside but on the inside are full of the bones of the dead and everything unclean. 28In the same way, on the outside you appear to people as righteous but on the inside you are full of hypocrisy and wickedness.

²⁹"Woe to you, teachers of the law and Pharisees, you hypocrites! You build tombs for the prophets and decorate the graves of the righteous. ³⁰And you say, 'If we had lived in the days of our ancestors, we would not have taken part with them in shedding the blood of the prophets.' ³¹So you testify against yourselves that you are the descendants of those who murdered the prophets. ³²Go ahead, then, and complete what your ancestors started!

³³"You snakes! You brood of vipers! How will you escape being condemned to hell? ³⁴Therefore I am sending you prophets and sages and teachers. Some of them you will kill and crucify; others you will flog in your synagogues and pursue from town to town. ³⁵And so upon you will come all the righteous blood that has been shed on earth, from the blood of righteous Abel to the blood of Zechariah son of Berekiah, whom you murdered between the temple and the altar. ³⁶Truly I tell you, all this will come on this generation."[10]

10. Matthew 23:13–36

PART I

1

The Truth

CHANCES ARE IF YOU'RE reading this, you're familiar with the historical figures who go unnamed in the previous story. The lowly wanderers represent
the disciples and their leader, Jesus. The religious leaders are the Pharisees
and Sadducees, the high priests of the day.

Chances also have it you hold a grudge against the religious leaders.
Unlike those in the crowds that day, we know the outcome of those ancient
happenings. We know Jesus would die at the hands of the religious leaders
and rise from the grave to prove his claim of deity as the Son of God. We
know Jesus' death on the cross brought God's kingdom to earth. We know
Jesus died for our own sins so we may be made holy in sight of God. We
also know it was the religious leaders who orchestrated Jesus' arrest and
subsequent execution. Due to what we know today, it's only natural for us
to hold them in great disdain.

Entertain the idea for a moment that you don't know how the story
ends. If you must go back and re-read the introduction, do so. In fact, I
highly encourage you to do so as names were left out for a reason. The
only difference in reading this time is this: leave your bias against the
Pharisees here.

See the scene from the eyes of someone present in the moment, watching the scene unfold before them. As the scenarios below will illustrate, it's
much more likely there was an opposite bias in the crowds that day—this is
the bias you should hold while reading the story told in the introduction.
This is the bias which will be built upon throughout this book as we learn

the true nature of the Pharisees. It's this bias which will eventually allow us to see why Jesus went unrecognized by those ancient figures, whereas now we can't fully comprehend how he was missed.

❧ ❧

Once again, you are present in the crowds of the temple courtyards as the sun sets behind the temple's looming walls. The difference is this time you have no idea what's going on amid the chaos of the Passover festival in Jerusalem. All you know is you are hot and exhausted and can't wait to settle into your camp for the night to finally give your legs a desperately needed break. One of your children is whining about being hungry from days of traveling on light rations and all they want is to eat from the local vendor stalls. They continuously tug on your hand the way kids do, but there's a commotion somewhere close which keeps you from turning your focus to them. The tugs become increasingly violent in nature and it takes everything in you to not give in and be led to one of the many smoked lamb stalls. After all, the scents wafting through the air are as savory as they've ever been. And if we're being honest, you're hungry too, but it's more important to have money to buy the traditional sacrifices than to make sure one's self is adequately fed. It appears each year the prices for the animals to sacrifice becomes more and more outrageous. To top it off and making matters worse, the exchange rate from your home currency to a shekel is increasing, causing you to not be able to buy as much as you have in years past.

Whereas once you were proud to offer up a flawless lamb for the Passover sacrifice, these days you settle for two doves—a less respected but still legally accepted form of a sin offering.[1] As it is, this financial lesson is one you know is important to teach your child at this age to engrain it in their minds for life—*it's more important to appease the temple and its officials than to satisfy one's own needs.*

Once again, something about the curiosity of the crowd eventually draws your attention away from your needy child and your own pangs of hunger. Taking your child by the arm, you meander closer through the center of the throng to find a peculiar situation unfolding. The men who accept and offer up your sacrifices each visit here are gathered around each other

---

1. Leviticus 5:7 says, "Anyone who cannot afford a lamb is to bring two doves or two young pigeons to the Lord as a penalty for their sin—one for a sin offering and the other for a burnt offering." Also repeated in Lev 12:8.

with an uneasiness you're not accustomed to. Several of their faces you know from the times they've accepted your dove offerings even though you know they should've been rejected due to slight imperfections—had they not shown mercy, you would've been forced to buy yet another set of doves. Instead, these specific men listened and received your pleading to accept the less than perfect doves. They showed you compassion so you could have enough to feed your children throughout the duration of the festival.

They cut you slack when they didn't have to. They did not use their position to extract more gain from your misfortune, as they easily could've done and have allegedly done so before. As such, you hold a sense of gratitude towards them.

From where you stand, the source of their uneasiness appears to be coming from a rough looking group of about a dozen men.

Who are these men? Prisoners? No, they're not in chains.

Homeless beggars, perhaps? Probably not as they look decently fed.

Then who the heck are they? What have these strangers done to upset the men you know? Whatever it is, they should be punished for it . . .

Which is a bizarre thought for you as you're consciously aware you have no basis for the predispositions now flooding your mind. Either way, your attention is heightened now and everything else will have to wait until this situation diffuses.

☙ ❧

Maybe this is a trek you've been making annually for as long as you can remember.[2] One of the religious leaders standing now at the center of the crowds has watched you grow up and shown you special attention throughout the years. He noticed something in you as a child and his place in society, along with his interest in you has given you a great sense of pride and honor. He has spent time teaching you how to worship God away from the temple, something your ancestors were never blessed with. He has always been a mentor and supporter, and you hold him in the highest regard. In fact, you were just walking into the court to say hello after yet another year apart.

You remind yourself you mustn't also forget to thank him, for his reference is likely the reason for your undeserved promotion back home.

2. Deuteronomy 16:16 says, "Three times a year all your men must appear before the LORD your God at the place he will choose: at the Festival of Unleavened Bread, the Festival of Weeks and the Festival of Tabernacles."

Part I

The reach of power of this man seemingly has no bounds, and you know sometimes he needs only to say the word to make something happen. Each year you look forward to hearing what he's learned in the last year so he can impart even more wisdom onto you. Lastly, his caring presence for you makes you feel special in front of the crowds.

What you find in the court is extremely unusual. The look on his face is stern and not the normal gentleness you're familiar with. You trace his gaze across the crowd to where it rests upon a ragged-looking man.

What is this? You think to yourself. *Another beggar here to interrupt your teacher's lessons. As if this hasn't happened enough in the past.*

The trust which has been long developed between yourself and the Pharisee causes you to inherently greatly distrust—and even despise—the stranger and his worn-and-torn band of scrubs.

What have they done to anger your Rabbi? Do they intend to harm him?

In your mind, your teacher needs only to say the word and you will not hesitate to mob them, for your loyalty without hindrance resides with the religious leaders.

❧ ❧

Maybe your parents were one of the 2,000 people who were crucified in the last revolt nearly 30 years ago when a local bandit's son, Judas, sacked Sepphoris.[3] Your parents were swayed by Judas' courage and joined him as he and his followers attacked the treasury and armory. For a short time they celebrated; however the Romans quickly took back the city and forced you to watch as both of your parents were nailed to a cross and suffocated to death, leaving you an orphan.[4] It was a horrible thing to witness at such a young age, and it taught you what happens if you dissent against Roman rule.

Nearly a decade later, you recall hearing about yet another rebel named Judas. You remember the poor Jewish folks who were swayed by Judas' teachings claiming the Roman taxes were too much and they could make a stand against Rome by not paying taxes.[5] It wasn't long before Rome found Judas and had him executed in the most brutal and humiliating manner possible: crucifixion.

3. "Sepphoris," Livius, 2017.
4. O'Reilly and Dugard, *Killing Jesus*, Page 75.
5. O'Reilly and Dugard, *Killing Jesus*, Page 92.

Not easily forgotten is what also happened to this Judas' two sons—they attempted vengeance for their late father, but failed and suffered the same gruesome fate.[6] As you learned at much too young an age, Judas' sons are just another example of wanna-be-heroes who died a criminal's death.

Nevertheless, once again you've heard rumors of a new king and his followers—that they too are going to rebel against the Romans and establish a Jewish kingdom. However, you've witnessed firsthand what happens to Jews who don't know their place when they rebel. The mere recollections are enough to terrify you and you refuse to suffer the same fate as your parents for someone else's rebellion. The images you've longed since suppressed cruelly meander their way to your conscience—your parents screaming in agony, desperately reneging on their anti-Roman views. They were told if they admitted their errors and swore allegiance to Caesar they would be spared. In the end, all their pitiable appeals earned them was several earth-shattering blows to their legs, causing them to break and leading them to suffocate in a quicker manner.

They made you watch. Those sick, sick soldiers.

As it is, you have been pre-dispossessed to know to stay far away from those with ill-fated dreams of freedom from Romans.

As you frequently voice to your friends amongst their constant complaints, *"anyone who stands against the Romans can count me out."*

When you enter the courtyard and find people hovering around a commotion, you only give it enough time to take a mental image of the apparent leader of the dirty strangers. One interesting thing that you notice is that he doesn't even appear to be speaking against the Romans, but is instead berating the religious leaders.

What?

The only rebellion less likely to fail against the Romans is a rebellion rooted in a civil war.

Unbelievable, the people protecting you from Roman execution are now going to be the ones who want you crucified. Smart thinking, pal.

The mental image you captured at this moment will stay with you forever, because, one way or another, exactly what you've imagined here is going to come to pass; except it turns out to have more implications for the world than any other moment in history.

༄ ༄

6. O'Reilly and Dugard, *Killing Jesus*, Page 91 & 93.

These scenarios may seem far-fetched. However it was far more likely these experiences were shared by most people in the crowd that day—whereas none share our experience. The crowd in the temple courts did not know what Jesus had come to do. It's certain these stories were shared by more people than those who believed Jesus was the Son of God. Sure, Jesus had performed miracles at this point in his life, but other prophets of old had also performed miracles.[7]

However, Jesus' ultimate claim of deity wasn't proven until he was to rise from the grave after three days.

As it was during the time, Jesus' own disciples didn't understand what he was really here to do. The people who deeply knew him and spent the most time with him didn't understand the significance of Jesus' life until he rose from the dead. Therefore, it's critical to understand the stories of Jesus' life from someone with the cultural perspective of the day and age.

Place yourselves in the shoes of one of the characters mentioned, or even make up your own. Take yourself back to the hot and dry day as the sun finally begins to fall behind the temple walls. The turmoil is overwhelming as people rub and brush against all sides, magnifying the already radiating heat. Somewhere across the way, something interesting is happening and the commotion draws the attention of everyone.

Now go back and reread the introduction.

❧ ❧

And you're back.

Immediately following Jesus' dramatic conclusion in Matthew 23:33–36, Matthew records the following: "Jesus left the temple and was walking away..."[8]

Jesus had just dropped the mic. I imagine Jesus finished his speech amid a deafening silence as the crowd and Pharisees digested what they had just heard. The crowds probably parted for Jesus as he inaudibly, yet assuredly, walked away to spend time with the Father.

---

7. Moses parted the Red Sea in Exodus 14:21–31. Elijah revived the widow of Zarephath's son in 1 Kings 17:17–24. Jonah is rescued from the belly of a fish in Jonah 1:17—2:10. Elisha revives the Shunammite woman's sons in 2 Kings 4:18–37. Daniel is rescued from the lion's den in Daniel 6:10–23.

8. Matthew 24:1

We are told by Matthew that the disciples came running up to him after he had left the temple and was walking away (likely to Bethany where he was staying at Lazarus' house).[9]

How did the disciples find themselves so far behind Jesus they had to catch up to him? *They must have stayed back after Jesus left.*

What were the disciples doing behind after Jesus left?

They likely shared the same astonishment as the crowd and were trying to diffuse a dire situation involving a group of incensed Pharisees. As we will discuss throughout this book, the Pharisees and other religious leaders to whom Jesus directed his rebukes would have found great offense at Jesus' words. They would likely have responded to Jesus in an uproar.

As for Jesus' disciples, they believed Jesus was a king, but they didn't yet know the purpose Jesus had come to Earth to fulfill. They didn't understand the type of king that he was, as they had only experienced one type of king in their lives—earthly kings. They, like the rest of the Jewish nation, were waiting on a king to deliver them from Roman rule and to establish an earthly kingdom. They would have known that establishing something like this would certainly require a united effort from the Jews—poor, rich, and educated alike.

However, their leader (and apparent best chance at achieving this unification) had just told the most popular and respected religious leaders in Jerusalem they were going to hell. Needless to say, this was not what the disciples had in mind for the unity of the nation.

The disciples may have stayed back trying to convince the Pharisees Jesus didn't really mean what he said. Maybe they were diffusing what was quickly becoming a mob. (It wouldn't be the first time a mob had formed with the intent on killing Jesus.[10])

Whatever the disciples were trying to accomplish back in the temple courts, it didn't work—unbeknownst to them, their teacher now only has a few days to live.

∽ ∾

9. John 12:1 tells us, "Six days before the Passover, Jesus came to Bethany, where Lazarus lived, whom Jesus had raised from the dead."

10. In Luke 4:29, we are told "[the people of Nazareth] got up, drove him out of the town, and took him to the brow of the hill on which the town was built, in order to throw him off the cliff." In John 8:59 we hear of another attempt at stoning Jesus: "At this, they picked up stones to stone him, but Jesus hid himself, slipping away from the temple grounds."

Part I

As you have likely begun to understand, a pivotal part of this book is to show how the Pharisees of ancient history were regarded in a much different manner than we hold them today. To this extent, it's accurate to presume unless a person has spent extensive time studying ancient Judaism and historical texts, we have no idea who the Pharisees truly were. The gospels do not give us an unbiased and accurate description of who they were and the role they played in the development of Judaism.

The word "Pharisee" today is used as an adjective describing someone who is hypocritical.[11] In ancient times, however, the word was a pronoun describing a sect of Jewish religious leaders.[12] In fact, the word was used in a positive connotation due to the role and contribution of the Pharisees.

There were several sects of Judaism during Jesus' day. The most widely known being the Sadducees, Essenes, Zealots, and the Pharisees. At the core of each of these sects were several fundamental beliefs:

1. belief in a single God,

2. belief in the covenant this God made with the Israelites,

3. and the belief this covenant was recorded in the books written by Moses which make up the Torah.[13]

A pillar of this covenant involved numerous rules and regulations regarding a certain code of purity and holiness. While codes of purity and holiness are common in cultures around the world, the zeal and extent of the codes followed by the Jews set them apart in their fervor. Roman emperor Tiberius was fascinated by Jewish customs and traditions and he found Jews to be some of the most devout subjects of Rome. In a letter to Pontius Pilate regarding how to treat Jews, he wrote: "change nothing already sanctioned by custom, but to regard as a sacred trust both the Jews themselves, and their laws, which are conducive to public order."[14]

Apart from these fundamental beliefs, each sect had their own methods for interpretation and practice making them unique from other sects.[15] This type of branching is not exclusive to history and can be noted in modern Christian denominations: Protestants, Evangelicals, Baptists, etc.

---

11. "Pharisee: Definition of Pharisee by Lexico," Lexico Dictionaries.

12. John M Cunningham, "Pharisee," Encyclopædia Britannica.

13. Petri Merenlahti, "Judaism in the Time of Jesus."

14. O'Reilly and Dugard, *Killing Jesus*, Page 130.

15. Merenlahti, "Judaism in the Time of Jesus."

ᑐᑌ ᑐᑌ

The Pharisaical sect represented a political and religious party of Jews who believed in adherence to both the Written Law (*Torah*) and Oral Law as a means of salvation.[16] This contrasted with the other main Jewish sects because the others only believed in the written Law of Moses (*also known at the Torah, the Law of Moses represents the biblical books of Genesis, Exodus, Leviticus, Numbers, and Deuteronomy*). The most commonly-known sect apart from the Pharisees, the Sadducees left no room for interpretation of the laws contained in these books. We would refer to them today as being very "legalistic."

Before the Pharisees came onto the scene, it's believed the power in the Jewish religion resided within the aristocratic sect of the Sadducees. Alleged to come from descendants of Zadok, the high priest during the time of Solomon,[17] the Sadducees were made up of priests and other wealthy relations. Ancient tradition held that only Zadok's descendants were truly pious and could perform the priestly duties of the temple.[18] Subsequently, they were the ones who could afford the opulent temple sacrifices and they excluded the common people from any sort of decision making regarding the practicing of their faith.[19] The Sadducees were much more conservative than the Pharisees and "stressed the importance of the priests in the Temple cult, while the Pharisees insisted on the participation of all Jews."[20]

The image this creates is one of inclusion in Jewish culture. The long ancestral line of priests and their wealthy families had held the power and control of Judaism both in and outside the temple.

This type of power can be illustrated using the following example.

A person became unclean if they encountered something deemed "unclean" by the various laws found in the Torah.[21] Those who were deemed unclean were avoided and outcasted until they became clean again.[22] (*The various processes of becoming clean are also found in the Torah.*)

16. Merenlahti, "Judaism in the Time of Jesus."

17. 1 Kings 1:39 and 1 Chronicles 6:4–8.

18. "Sadducees," Livius, 1996.

19. "Ancient Jewish History: Pharisees, Sadducees & Essenes," Jewish Virtual Library.

20. "Sadducees," Livius, 1996.

21. Numbers 19:22 says, "Anything that an unclean person touches becomes unclean, and anyone who touches it becomes unclean till evening."

22. Leviticus 7:21 reads, "Anyone who touches something unclean—whether

Most of the time this required being examined by a priest who would review various statutes as outlined in the Torah. If the person could be cleared by them, the priest could then render something which was originally unclean, clean again. As mentioned before, the priests were the Sadducees.

Imagine someone coming on the scene who threatened the Sadducees' teachings—this person was deemed unclean and that was the end of it. They were outcast and avoided and any power and influence they once enjoyed would quickly fade.[23] Any followers amassed by this individual would have two options:

1. stick with their teacher and endure a similar exile from society or

2. rebuke their teacher and submit to the authority of the Sadducees.

Both options brought about the same result, and those who challenged authority were dealt with decisively and permanently—such was life for those living in ancient Israel in the centuries building up to the arrival of Jesus.

In the second century BCE, the Pharisees came on the scene supposing life outside the temple was also meant to be lived in worship to God. Their studies led them to propose God was to be worshipped at the temple and at home, in the streets and at mealtime. While this is commonplace today, this was a radical new teaching at the time.

For the last several centuries, the Sadducees had regarded the temple as the only place where God could be worshipped by practicing Jews. As such, those wishing to worship God had no choice but to visit the temple, which conveniently involved paying taxes and purchasing sacrifices (*to and from whom? The Sadducees*).

While people would still need to visit the temple regularly for the annual three festivals, the Pharisees' belief in the interpretation of the written law brought about a slight power shift down the societal ladder. The

---

human uncleanness or an unclean animal or any unclean creature that moves along the ground—and then eats any of the meat of the fellowship offering belonging to the Lord must be cut off from their people."

23. John 9:22 gives us insight into the political and economic ruin which came from being put out of the synagogue. When Jesus healed the blind man, the Jewish leaders went to his parents and asked him how their son was born blind but could now see. Rather than acknowledge Jesus as the Messiah, the parents told the leaders to ask their son themselves. This was to avoid being outcast from the synagogue, which is what happened to those who acknowledged Jesus as the Messiah.

Sadducees had only allowed their own a place in the temple cult. Now, because of the Pharisees, all Jews were able to participate. The Pharisees came from a lower social class than the Sadducees, which in and of itself provided a fresh breath to the long-oppressed common folk. However, they didn't stop at just common folk and their teachings and practices further included others who were once excluded.[24]

How radical! It sounds like what our Messiah did during his life.

The Pharisees were much more progressive in their teachings and practice and they quickly amassed a large, passionate following and secured their place in the temple and history books. Petri Merenlahti provides insight into this when he writes the Pharisees taught, *"by observing the purity code every member of the people of God might participate in the holiness of God."*[25] The Sadducees' beliefs had only allowed themselves the ability to participate in the holiness of God, excluding anyone who wasn't part of their ranks.

Understanding the human psyche allows us to glean from this the true extent of popularity of the Pharisees during their time. Not only can we presume their inclusivity increased their admiration by the people, but we can also hint at their popularity from the way history has kept their name. History remembers those who have profound influences on others. Of the varying sects of Judaism during Jesus' day, the Pharisees are the most commonly discussed and recognized group of the rest. This is not to say the other groups weren't important, but they did not match the prominence, significance, and popularity of the Pharisees to whom Jesus addressed on that day.

The following example is used to illustrate how the Pharisees came to be viewed as revolutionaries apart from the Sadducees. The written law states an eye for an eye must be paid for in punishment.

"But if there is harm, then you shall pay life for life, eye for eye, tooth for tooth, hand for hand, foot for foot, burn for burn, wound for wound, stripe for stripe."[26]

If the actions of one person caused the loss of an eye in another, the Sadducees saw that the original perpetrator would have their own eye removed. This restricted form of thinking was not shared by the Pharisees. The Pharisees' views allowed for interpretation of this law and they came

24. Joshua Garroway, "Pharisees."

25. Petri Merenlahti, "Judaism in the Time of Jesus."

26. Exodus 21:23–25

to hold that it may not particularly require the removal of the eye itself, but rather something worth the value of an eye. This could've amounted to an agreed-upon sum of money or equally valued parcel of land. The idea and object of value was open to interpretation. These principles were not only applied to situations involving injury, but rather they applied this type of sophisticated thinking to all aspects of life, worship, and the laws of Moses.

Furthermore, the Pharisees were incredibly gifted intellectuals. All it takes is one glance at the pages of recordings and thoughts collected in the Talmud to make this clear. The Talmud—accumulated over centuries of writings and debates—is in essence the oral law in written form. (The Talmud will be explored further in Chapter 7.) While the Talmud was not written and compiled until the Second Century CE, its teachings and recordings give insight into the thinking of the Pharisees during Jesus' day and before he walked the earth.

Encompassing thousands of pages of text, the Talmud attempts to explore any and all scenarios involving the hundreds of laws found in the Torah. This attention to detail and focus on evolving the Jewish faith is summarized by Wellhausen when he writes, "Thus, the Pharisees are not distinguished from the people through the peculiar content of their will, but through the degree of zeal and their consistency in the common aspirations of the citizens of the holy community."[27]

Even excluding the Talmud from the discussion, there is still a lot of information to dissect here in order to fully understand how radical the teachings of the Pharisees were relative to the principles of the day. Several key points to take away and remember are these:

1. the Pharisees included all Jews in the practice of worshipping God, whereas they had once been excluded by the Sadducees,

2. the Pharisees were progressive thinkers compared to other Jewish sects,

3. and the Pharisees encouraged the worship of God to also include life outside the temple walls.

As you have likely begun to comprehend, the men described above appear to be much different than who we've come to believe them to be.

---

27. Julius Wellhausen and Mark Edward. Biddle, *The Pharisees and the Sadducees*, pg 15.

They were the voice of the common people and they had included those who were once excluded. This was something to be celebrated as their progressiveness paved the way for more people to learn about and worship God. Furthermore, their reasons for being proud of their accomplishments seemed to be rooted in Scripture.

Psalm 82:3-4 reads, "Defend the weak and the fatherless; uphold the cause of the poor and the oppressed. Rescue the weak and the needy; deliver them from the hand of the wicked."

Leviticus 19:15 says, "Do not pervert justice; do not show partiality to the poor or favoritism to the great, but judge your neighbor fairly."

Isaiah 61:1 reads, "The Spirit of the Sovereign Lord is on me, because the Lord has anointed me to proclaim good news to the poor. He has sent me to bind up the brokenhearted, to proclaim freedom for the captives and release from darkness for the prisoners."

There are dozens and dozens of other verses which only expand upon that which the Pharisees believed—they had earned the right to be proud of what they had done. They had earned the right to reap the benefits of their work. They had earned the respect and admiration of the people.

As we will continuously expand upon, further reflection and analysis leads to a more detailed picture emerging as to who they were. Contrary to the way they are portrayed in the gospels, the Pharisees weren't evil men trying to murder the holiest man to ever live.

Instead, they were progressive men who altered the practice of Judaism for the good of the common people—who also happened to be threatened by everything taught by a lowly carpenter from Nazareth.

Jesus' teachings threatened to directly anger and lead to involvement by the Romans.

The Pharisees had evolved a faith where common people could find themselves closer to the One true God without offending Roman rule. They created safety for the Jews under Roman rule and this was something to be celebrated. They were men eagerly trying to protect the people against an even more radical set of teachings which—in their minds—threatened them and the entire Jewish nation.

The gospels record this discussion amongst the Pharisees and other religious leaders.

"If we let him go on like this, everyone will believe in him, and then the Romans will come and take away both our temple and our nation."[28]

---

28. John 11:48

When I view the Pharisees from this lens of what they had done and what they were trying to save, I can't help but believe I have a lot in common with them. I know the way I inherently react when something foreign interrupts the safety I've created in my everyday life.

Things that threaten my everyday routine can't possibly compare to the potential dangers to the Jewish nation if they angered the Roman rulers. Such things in my life may jeopardize my influence, or at worst, my job. However, nothing in my life threatens to compare to the potential devastation possible at the hands of the Romans. The Romans had the ability and power to erase an entire nation, and the Pharisees were doing and would continue to do everything in their power to keep that from happening. They were acting as protectors of the Jewish people, God's chosen Nation.

How is it that men who at one point appear to have so much in common with the teachings of Jesus become to be viewed as arch-nemesis of Jesus?

As the Bible consistently shows, humans—while for a time may find themselves in righteousness with God—will always fall away from him without the constant practice of repentance and submission and constant relationship. The Pharisees, while they would have liked to believe otherwise, were no exception to this rule. It's imperative that we learn this "falling away" is part of our humanity. Without being aware of it, we are doomed to repeat it.

David was a man after God's own heart,[29] yet he had an affair with Bathsheba and had her husband killed.[30]

Samson was dedicated to God from the womb,[31] yet he indulged in prostitutes and was controlled by his own rage.[32]

Solomon was a wise ruler who loved the Lord,[33] yet he kept 700 wives and 300 concubines—clearly well beyond the single partner God commanded of the Israelites.[34]

Therefore, I'm led to reflect on this: Would I have acted differently than the Pharisees had I been in their shoes? Would I have trusted

29. 1 Samuel 13:14 mentions Samuel's words to Saul concerning David, "But now your kingdom will not endure; the Lord has sought out a man after his own heart and appointed him ruler of his people, because you have not kept the Lord's command."

30. David sent Uriah to the front lines where he was killed in battle. 2 Samuel 11:17.

31. Judges 13:5

32. In Judges 16:1, Samson sleeps with the prostitute Delilah. In Judges 15:8, Samson attacked the Philistines for his revenge and viciously slaughtered many of them.

33. 1 Kings 3:12

34. 1 Kings 11:3

a stranger who posed the greatest threat to my nation's very existence? *"Probably not."*

My fear and reluctance to be exposed to danger would have kept me from recognizing Jesus.

My knowledge of the Old Testament and what it tells me that God requires would have kept me from recognizing Jesus.

My pride would have kept me from seeing Jesus.

My desire to blend in with the crowds would have kept me from recognizing Jesus.

It's as simple and as complicated as this: My humanity would have kept me from recognizing Jesus.

By the time you have finished this book, I believe you will see how we are very much like the Pharisees.

2

The Question

A QUESTION THAT WAS posed to me years ago set into motion a series of events that have culminated in the pages you're now reading.

"If Jesus walked the Earth today as he did before, would you recognize him?"

As I believe most Christians would do, without blinking I responded, *"of course I would!"*

Following in the steps of men before me, I never second-guessed myself for weeks following that question until one day, as I was going about my business, I collided with the following revelation.

Jesus has already walked the Earth once, and he went completely unrecognized.

How did this happen?

The Son of God, Creator of Men, Author of the Universe, stepped down to live amongst his creation, and yet no one recognized him. When I say no one, I'm referring to 99.99 percent of people who lived during the time Jesus walked the earth. As for the other hundredth of a percent of people, there were a few who believed him—a tax collector, a handful of prostitutes, some homeless people, disabled people, a few lepers, and some really poor folks.

The educated, wealthy, middle class, Jews, Romans, Greeks, his family and friends, teachers of the law, Pharisees, Sadducees, Essenes, high priests, students, teachers, farmers, metal workers, merchants, guards, soldiers, governors, kings, shepherds, servants, slaves, leaders, scribes, laborers, architects, block layers, masons, carpenters, and innkeepers, for the most part, did not believe Jesus was who he said he was.

This notion led me to wonder, to which of those groups would I belong?

Would I belong to the minute handful of sinners who believed Jesus? Or would I reside within the category of the Rest of Humanity?

When I honestly answered that question, I knew something had to change.

How had this realization avoided me for so long?

My journey to find answers to these questions began in the ever-popular book of Job.

∽ ∾

The purpose of the following message using Job as a reference is meant to show our need for humility and I encourage you to seek it and to seek it urgently. I use the word urgently because humility is required to take what you need to take from this book.

Skimming over the pages of this book as if you already know everything about Jesus is not a good use of your time.

Skimming over the pages of this book because someone begged you to read it is not a good use of your time.

Skimming over the pages of this book without a genuine desire to deepen your understanding of the bible, as well as the teachings and personhood of Jesus, is not a good use of your time.

If any of these scenarios happen to be you, I'm going to propose you do yourself a favor, do me a favor, do your friends and family and spouse or future spouse and children or future children or in-laws or future in-laws or girlfriend or boyfriend or roommate or neighbor a favor. The favor is this—do not continue this book until you've become someone willing to learn from and place yourself in the shoes walked by Jesus and the Pharisees 2,000 years ago. Do not continue until you're ready to admit you may not know everything you think you know. Humility is required to understand where we fail and how we can move closer to Jesus. Humility is required to read this book and to understand how someone without a bible-college degree has something the Holy Spirit wants to use to help others see Jesus more clearly.

I am not only pointing the finger at you, the reader. Humility is also required on my behalf to understand I may have nothing to teach others, and it is possible no other eyes will see these words but mine. The humility I'm seeking is to be okay with understanding God is doing what brings God glory and if this is merely a lesson for myself, then so be it.[1]

～～

The book of Job is the first of the poetic books in the Hebrew Bible. While one could easily be led to believe the author is Job himself, others have suggested it may have been written by Moses, Solomon, or Elihu.

Whether the author is Job or not, the significance and lasting teachings from the book are crucial to understanding our place before God. A solid faith foundation is a byproduct of understanding the book of Job.

Written approximately 4000 years ago during the time of the Patriarchs (2000–1800 BCE), the book of Job tells the dramatic riches-to-rags and back-to-riches story of a farmer from Uz (Northeast Palestine, between Damascus and the Euphrates River).[2] Job was his name and faith was his game.

Sorry about that.

I'm not too sorry because from the very beginning we are told exactly who Job is: "This man was blameless and upright; he feared God and shunned evil."[3]

Another verse states: "He was the greatest man among all the people of the East."[4]

Job was not only a man of great faith, he was incredibly wealthy and prosperous, enjoying herds of 7,000 sheep, 3,000 camels, 500 oxen and 500 donkeys.[5] Aside from his animals, he had a large number of servants and a large family: 7 sons and 3 daughters.[6]

By the cultural standards of Jewish antiquity, Job had it all. He had numerous male heirs to continue his legacy and enough inheritance to ensure

1. I've wrestled with this and there have been weeks and months where I've set this book aside in order to discover if this is for me or for others. After being prompted multiple times to pick it back up and write, I'm more confident in the way God will use this. However, at the end of the day, I've watched God use the lessons within to mold and shape my life. So, even if I don't sell a single copy, this will all have been worth it because of the way I now see and relate to Jesus.

2. *Life Application Study Bible*, Page 762, Vital Statistics Notes.

3. Job 1:1

4. Job 1:3

5. Job 1:3

6. Job 1:2

each descendant was well sought after. Job had been blessed by God and this much was clear to those who knew him.

Unbeknownst to Job, Satan appears before the Lord and wages Job is only righteous because he's been continually blessed by God. Satan then contends if he is allowed to strip Job of his wealth and riches, Job will curse God and turn from him.[7]

God takes him up on this offer. God allows Satan to tempt Job with only one pitfall: Satan is not allowed to kill Job. This fails to be a positive outcome for Job and soon becomes Job's biggest complaint about his life—that he is still alive.[8]

Satan gets to work. Immediately, Job's family is killed when their house collapses from strong winds. His servants are killed by the neighboring Sabeans after they steal Job's oxen and donkeys. His herds are killed by raiding Chaldeans. He soon falls deathly ill and his body becomes covered with painful sores.[9] Job went from having it all—a beautiful family and wealth—to nothing at all.

His status was gone, his legacy was gone, he was an outcast, and shortly afterwards, abandoned by his own wife. This kind of thing didn't just happen to those God loved, as would be discussed and debated in over 90 percent of the book.

Job has three friends who mourn with him for seven days without speaking—Eliphaz the Temanite, Bildad the Shuhite, and Zophar the Naamathite.[10] For seven days they sat there silently while Job mourned.[11] There was nothing they could say to him to ease his suffering, and they knew it.

Finally Job speaks, his words flowing out from deep within as molten rock from the ocean's grand trenches. He mourns as deep runs to deep.

"Why is light given to those in misery, and life to the bitter of soul, to those who long for death that does not come, who search for it more than for hidden treasure, who are filled with gladness and rejoice when they reach the grave?"[12]

---

7. Job 1:11

8. Job 3:11

9. Job 2:7

10. Job 2:11–12

11. Jewish tradition held that people who comforted mourners should not speak until the one who mourns speaks first.

12. Job 3:20–22

Job's discourse proceeds as he proclaims his innocence and continues to praise God; yet he never cedes guilt to his friends who claim he must have sinned to deserve the ways he's been punished. Eliphaz the Temanite claims Job is suffering because he has sinned.[13] Bildad the Shuhite tells Job it's because he won't admit he has sinned.[14] Zophar the Naamathite says Job's sins deserve even more punishment than he's received.[15]

Through it all, Job stands his ground; for he knows he is blameless. In chapter 31 Job describes his blamelessness. (Not direct quote)

> *"Father, I do not contend to question your holiness, but I do not deserve what you have allowed to happen to me. I do not look at young women with lust. I have always walked in honesty and integrity. I have not allowed my heart to pursue another woman than my wife. I have not denied my servants justice. I have given to the poor and served widows and orphans. I have been generous with my wealth and have never idolized it. I have loved my enemies. I have opened my doors to the homeless. I will stand up for every decision I have made for I know my steps have been blameless for all my days."*

The bottom line is this—Job doesn't deserve what has happened to him. Yet, for some reason which is hard to fathom, he still praises God and refuses to curse his name.

How many of us could do the same in Job's shoes? How many of us could face the loss and destruction Job faced and still give glory to God?

I have been one to get angry at God for a bad day at work.

I have been angry at God over a failed direct message.

I have been angry at God over the most simple and fleeting and trivial trials.

Yet, here was Job who could stand before God, having lost everything, and still give God praise.

Finally, after a fourth friend of Job named Elihu contends that God is righteous and Job is not and, therefore, his suffering doesn't have to make sense, God speaks to Job.

God speaks to him from a storm. *"Who is this that obscures my plans with words without knowledge? Brace yourself like a man; I will question you, and you shall answer me."*[16]

---

13. Job 4:7–8
14. Job 8:2–7
15. Job 11:6–12
16. Job 38:2

For the next two chapters, God poses questions to Job.

"Where were you when I laid the earth's foundations?"[17]

"Have you ever given orders to the morning, or shown the dawn its place?"[18]

"Have you journeyed to the springs of the sea or walked in the recesses of the deep?"[19]

"Have you entered the storehouses of the snow, or seen the storehouses of the hail, which I reserve for times of trouble?"[20]

"Can you bind the chains of the Pleiades? Can you loosen Orion's belt?"[21]

"Do you send the lightning bolts on their way? Do they report to you?"[22]

"Who gives the ibis wisdom, or gives the rooster understanding?"[23]

"Do you know when the mountain goats give birth? Do you watch when the doe bears her fawn?"[24]

"Do you count the months till they bear? Do you know the time they give birth?"[25]

"Who let the wild donkey go free? Who untied its ropes?"[26]

"Do you give the horse its strength or clothe its neck with a flowing mane?"[27]

"Does the hawk take flight by your wisdom and spread its wings towards the south?"[28]

"Does the eagle soar at your command and build its nest on high?"[29]

⚬⚬

17. 38:4
18. 38:12
19. 38:16
20. 38:22
21. 38:31
22. 38:35
23. 38:36
24. 39:1
25. 39:2
26. 39:5
27. 39:19
28. 39:26
29. 39:27

Job was a holy man, a blameless man. I am a sinner. Yet Job's response was to shut his mouth in reverence to God's sovereignty. "*I am unworthy— how can I reply to you? I put my hand over my mouth. I spoke once but have no answer—twice, but I will say no more.*"[30]

To understand we don't understand God and he is infinitely greater than anything we can imagine is essential to knowing him. Not only was Job both blameless and righteous, he was also humble enough to understand his place before God. Job is the ideal model for us. As the book of Job teaches us, we don't need to know why God does what he does, and it doesn't need to make sense to us.

I fear the significance of this was not merely lost on just the Pharisees, but also on us today. How do we handle being asked "why does God allow bad things to happen to good people?" How do we handle the question "what about evolution?" How do dinosaur and Neanderthal bones dating to 100,000 years ago fit into the biblical picture?

More than simply questions posed to us, how do we react when the happenings in our life don't make sense? Why was the pastor's daughter taken too soon? Why can't we have kids? Why did the sickness happen to the one we love? Why can't I get out of this overwhelming depression? Why was the military pilot taken in a training accident? Why were *they* taken from this earth during a robbery gone wrong? Why are children exposed to such evil and human trafficking throughout the world? Why were they taken advantage of at such a young age? Why were they in the wrong place at the wrong time? Why is this happening to me? Why was I forced to go through something like that? Why did I have to watch someone I love go through what they did? Why am I still alone? Why me? Why them?

Take note of what Job had before and what he has at this point in his life. If there's ever been a human being with the resume or curriculum vitae to respond to God, it's Job. Except Job doesn't respond as I would were I in his shoes; Job doesn't respond the way *we* would.

Even after Job has already humbled himself the first time, God speaks again. In response to God's second discourse, Job humbles himself even further. He leaves what he believed to be his wisdom at his feet.

"*1 Then Job replied to the Lord: 2 "I know that you can do all things; no purpose of yours can be thwarted. 3 You asked, 'Who is this that obscures my plans without knowledge?' Surely I spoke of things I did not understand, things too wonderful for me to know. 4 "You said, 'Listen now, and I will speak;*

30. Job 40:4–5

I will question you, and you shall answer me.' [5]*My ears had heard of you but now my eyes have seen you.* [6]*Therefore I despise myself and repent in dust and ashes."*[31]

Job has finally grasped what it's imperative for humans to understand. Job finally comprehends it's impossible for him to understand the wonderful vastness of God. It's out of this comprehension of God's immensity that Job submits himself and repents for his unknowingly dumbfounded accusations.

What this passage really teaches us is how we, as human beings, don't know much of anything. No matter how wise we believe ourselves to be, we will always have infinitely more to learn when it comes to our understanding of God and humanity.[32] The wisdom God has blessed us with is not for condemning others or for holding ourselves in high esteem. Any wisdom we've been blessed with is a mere gift to be used to instruct others and will sporadically be the case to rebuke friends, but only out of love for them, rather than pursuing our own desires and agendas.

The story of Job is one of humility. This story and this lesson were lost on the Pharisees and teachers of the law. This is part of the reason that when their Savior came, they didn't recognize him. The God they spent their entire life studying about and praying to and fasting for, stood right in front of them as a man and they killed him.

I am not smarter than the Pharisees. I am not a tenth as righteous as Job and I'm not entirely sure the goal is to gain the wisdom of the Pharisees and the righteousness of Job. The goal is to understand it's impossible for us to achieve our place before God. Only Jesus could do that for us, and that's why we love him so much. If I love him so much, I want to be able to recognize him if he is physically here today.

Luckily for me, he is. He's not always physically visible, but nevertheless here, and I don't want to miss him any more than I already have.

For that to happen, I must fix what's been broken and misunderstood in the days from my birth until now. If we are unable to learn from the past, history is doomed to repeat itself. The studied philosopher George

---

31. Job 42:1–6

32. Writing about Israel's history in First Corinthians 10:12, Paul warns, "So, if you think you are standing firm, be careful that you don't fall!" His warning is a dramatic attempt to keep people from thinking they have it figured out. This same teaching must be applied to our understanding of God and our humanity.

Santayana once said, "Those who cannot remember the past are doomed to repeat it."[33]

I no longer want the wisdom I've thought I've possessed. Instead, I want real, Godly wisdom, which starts with humility and knowing nothing.[34] I don't want the righteousness of Job, but instead the humility he possesses. This humility is one which cannot be a one-time reckoning. This must become a way of living, of reminding oneself daily of the inferiority of our humanity in comparison to the infinity of God. As Job says in Job 42:6, we must despise ourselves and repent in dust and ashes.

As soon as we think we have something figured out, we must be ready to throw it into the wind and accept teaching. Our inability to accept correction will only cause us to further resemble the Pharisees. Our lack of willingness to accept correction will lead us into the same spiritual blindness which inhibited them from seeing who Jesus was when he stood before them.

If Job can humble himself before God, we must be willing to do the same. If Job can leave his wisdom behind him and step into deeper Godly wisdom, we must be willing to do the same.

We must relearn everything we thought we knew.

"The only true wisdom is in knowing you know nothing."

—SOCRATES

---

33. George Santayana was a twentieth-century English philosopher. He received his PhD from Harvard and later returned to the school to teach philosophy to storied students such as T. S. Eliot, Robert Frost, and W. E. B. Du Bois.

34. James 3:17 says wisdom is this: "But the wisdom that comes from heaven is first of all pure; then peace-loving, considerate, *submissive*, full of mercy and good fruit, impartial and sincere." (Emphasis own)

3

Going Back to Move Forward

IN THE LAST 2,000 years, there has been a disconnect in understanding the relationship between Jesus and the Pharisees.

Contrary to the scenes depicted in the gospels, and the way many of us view the relationship today, Jesus did not hate the Pharisees.

Jesus did not hate people.

Jesus hated the sin of pride. Jesus hated the sin of self-righteousness. He hated the lack of humility expressed by the religious leaders. Jesus hated the sin that caused them to be blind to who he was. He hated standing in front of those he loved knowing they couldn't see him back.

Imagine the frustration of Jesus in these interactions with the Pharisees. He loves these people with such intensity he will shortly die a criminal's death to give everyone the opportunity to be redeemed back to God, except these men have been blinded by their sin and their pride and they can't see Jesus for who he is. Nor can they see the kingdom he brought to Earth.

Unfortunately for us, at some point or another we all will fall into the same trap. In order to resolve this problem, the root must be fixed. Until the foundational problem is understood and corrected, the problem will remain. Two truths that will help us reach the roots are these:

1. Things are not always what they seem.

2. We must go backwards before we can go forward.

Things are not often what they seem.

I have found this and continue to find this in common problems as well as philosophical topics. I am going to open up and share examples of this in my life. You may or may not relate, and some of them you may find trivial. Humor me, though, and do not pass judgement before you understand how radical the gaining of wisdom has been in these areas. The purpose of sharing excerpts from my life is to provide tangible examples with the hope you will be better equipped to apply these lessons to your own life.

Throughout my young adult years, I found myself in a multitude of relationships with women. As I progressed through my twenties, a similar cycle continued to repeat itself. Through the grace of Godly wisdom, I've finally been able to recognize and break the cycle in which I had been trapped in with regards to relationships.

This cycle would begin with meeting a girl. One way or another, I would get a hold of some form of contact. We would begin communicating sporadically and swiftly progress to nonstop interacting via multiple channels: in person, thru text, thru social media, etc.

It wouldn't take long for the relationship to progress from relative strangers to hanging out constantly and staying the night with each other. This sometimes happened in the course of two days. These were not always sexually intimate relationships, however sleeping in a bed with another being, minus the exception of family, is more often than not an emotionally intimate experience. This form of intimacy can be equally as dangerous for the soul as carnal intimacy.

This relationship progression would continue for a month or so until I started to lose interest. I would typically find something in their personality which irked me, and I supposed it to be a deal breaker. More common than this, though, I would meet another woman who offered something different. *Something new.*

I would start talking to the new woman with a similar enthusiasm as I had with the current one. Things would start slow and pick up progressively. Meanwhile, sadly, I would still be dating the first. It wouldn't be long before the courage I found at the bottom of the bottle resurrected itself as infidelity.

I would store my heartbreak over what I'd done, telling myself it had to happen that way for me to learn my lesson. Generally, I would end up being with neither woman as I had hurt one and I'd run from the other because they had been part of me causing someone else pain.

After a few weeks of self-reflection, I would be back at it again with a new girl, but this time would be different—or at least it's what I believed.

Sooner rather than later, the same thing would happen, except it progressively got worse. It wouldn't be only one other woman, there would be two, or three, or even four. The more times the cycle and pattern repeated, the more I needed to fill me up. I wasn't trying to fit the description of "player," but I was too focused on myself that I couldn't see what I was doing to others.

The craziest part about this entire thing is I didn't recognize the pattern until years later, when I irrevocably started stumbling upon some tangible wisdom.

During the half-decade this cycle was occurring, I thoroughly believed what I was looking for was going to be found in a woman. It was my belief that eventually one of these women would be the last, and thus the cycle would end. This is why my search was so relentless. I was fixated on finding someone which would end the cycle, except I didn't even know what I was searching for. I thought it would be a feeling, similar to what the movies portrayed as "when you know, you know."

As I've finally come to realize, this was far from the truth. I had erroneously attributed my fluctuating feelings to the woman not being the right one. If I kept searching, though, I would find the one which would solve my problem. As such, I chugged along from one woman to the next and to the next, wrecking their hearts—and gradually, but completely, mine in the process.

As you can imagine, things were not at all what they appeared to be.

Through my maturation and gaining of wisdom, I have come to understand the wolf in sheep's clothing. Those things I was searching for in a woman could not be found there, at least not permanently. Those first several weeks, things were exciting and new, but my solace was temporary. This was all it ever amounted to: temporary solace and nothing more; both a momentary and fleeting suppression of the inadequacy I felt.

What I couldn't comprehend at the time was that deep down I was searching to feel wanted. Past rejection had made me feel undesirable and I subconsciously sought to fill the void through women.

I was searching to end a deep loneliness. In my mind during this period, I believed being with someone would take away this deep sense of loneliness.

I was looking for joy—a joy I didn't possess on my own.

Part I

I was looking for intimacy—in the only place the internet had taught young boys like me to find it.

What I was looking for—as I've come to plainly understand—I would never find in a woman. In fact, I would never find it anywhere but in a relationship with Jesus.

When Jesus met the woman at the well, he promised her a living water where she'd never be thirsty again.[1] This woman believed Jesus meant physical, liquid water. Jesus meant something else, something much bigger.

I had to learn this the hard way.

We all must learn this one way or another.

Regrettably, this was not a singular reckoning for me.

During my college years, as the above story was unravelling itself, it's fair to say I frequented the bar scene sometimes two to three times a week. After years of binge drinking, I began to find myself oddly uncomfortable at the bars I regularly visited. It was an incredibly peculiar experience to watch myself devolve into loathing for something that I thought I loved.

It didn't change instantly where one day I woke up and decided I despised these bars. It was a manifestation of various emotions that would take place as I went about my unruly evenings.

The most conspicuous emotions were anxiousness and uneasiness. At first, I would merely solve this problem by consuming larger amounts of alcohol to suppress these feelings. One day a revelation, which I believed to be real wisdom, came to me: because I was now older and more mature, instead of hanging around college bars it was time to grow up and move on to the adult bars.

It felt so good to have finally figured it out.

I remember feeling as if a mountain had been lifted and thrown into the sea. I believed this moment to be rather monumental of sorts, a poignant ascent as I moved up my ranking into adulthood. Not only was I becoming more self-aware, but to believe I was leaving those sinking feelings behind for good was liberating.

Taking these revelations into account, off I went in my button-down-plaid shirt (with one more button than previously buttoned up); my mature and grown self, proud of my awareness and self-understanding.

As I would soon find out, concisely and with finality, things aren't always as they seem.

---

1. Story found in John 4:1–42.

Little did I know I was binge drinking to cover depression and a lifelong undiagnosed anxiety disorder.

Little did I know the current spiral was only the tip of the iceberg of the murky depths I would soon plunge.

Little did I know the final reckoning wouldn't occur until hopelessness would come to define my existence.

Little did I know . . . I hardly knew anything at all.

I wholeheartedly believed the problem was the atmosphere and maturity of the patrons of the bars I frequented.

However, the real problem was nothing close to this. The real problem could not be relieved by anything other than a personal relationship with Jesus. The real problem would nearly cost me my life by the time it was all said and done.

✐ ✐

The previous two examples have been used to show how I've seen this play out in the past. The following illustration is provided to demonstrate how I've once again watched this pertain to present day life. This lesson of things not always being what they seem is not only one to be recognized in past experiences, rather also to be applied moving forward.

✐ ✐

My brother and I flip and renovate houses. In my opinion, my brother doesn't work as hard as I do. In my opinion, he seems to prioritize everything else above working on our projects. Whether it be working out at the gym, binge watching *The Office*, or hanging out with friends, it appears everything else comes before working.

From where I see it, I often find myself working alone, muttering under my breath about how I'm being taken advantage of and how lazy I believe him to be. Whether I'm laying tile or making cuts and installing floors, I find a persistent internal dialogue.

How is he going to play me like this after everything I've done for him? He doesn't deserve my talents and abilities. How childish is he to focus on his physical appearance rather than preparing for the future? I've never been so deliberately unappreciated by anyone. How does someone get their priorities so out of whack! If only he actually knew who Jesus was, he would learn to focus on the right things.

This dialogue couldn't stay silent and I made sure to voice my displeasure at home where we live together. I've also made sure others know how I feel and that I'm the one doing the work while my brother finds every excuse not to.

This feeling of being taken advantage of and being treated unfairly has at times nearly crumbled our relationship.

After starting this book, I began to comprehend that this pattern of thought I've discovered in my past is probably not confined to the past.

Sure enough and once again, I discovered that things aren't always what they seem.

My anger towards my brother, which could slightly be validated, was rooted in something else—something more profound and gloomier.

The house we were remodeling was the first full house I've designed, from the bathrooms to the kitchen to the common areas. I poured time and effort into designing and redesigning, preparing layouts and quantities, and managing every aspect of what I proudly considered an efficient and attractively designed home.

I was seeking to finish the project quickly to receive validation from others that my work was good. To be validated that my work was special. To be validated that my talents were remarkably unique. This bottomless desire for validation and acknowledgement surpassed all else, and I was furious I didn't have it.

I channeled this anger onto my brother. This anger of not yet being validated led me to believe my brother was taking advantage of me. This anger nearly crumbled the closest relationship in my life.

I thought finishing the house would bring finality to this area. I thought finishing would bring me validation and that would change how I felt about my brother. However, I now see clearly it was just a ruse, yet another wolf in sheep's clothing to keep me from identifying the root of the problem.

While I believed the problem was being taken advantage of (and no one could've convinced me otherwise), it was instead an innate desire to be validated and receive affirmation from others. If those things happened, in my mind, then I would feel good. I would be happy.

Wow . . .

My attitude, disposition, and self-confidence rested on how many people affirmed my work instead of resting on the fact that Jesus rose from the dead after three days. It was built upon other peoples' thoughts of me instead of knowing Jesus died on the cross to bring me into eternal relation-ship with God.

One of these is fleeting and one is not . . . can you guess which one? Which is a more solid foundation to build your life upon?

As I take a step back, I can only imagine the dozens of other areas of my life this camouflage occurs. I will spare you countless more stories of how this has unfolded in my life and instead leave with this: *When you find things to be true about your past, the next place to look is your present.*

Things aren't always what they seem. We must learn to recognize the wolf in sheep's clothing. You can't trap a snipe (bird) if you don't know what it looks like. You can't repair a flat if you don't know what caused it. A math problem can't be solved with horoscopes (*I just offended a lot of you with this one*).

I can't begin to propose that I know where this might apply in your life: where things aren't what they seem. It may be in the way you relate to your parents. It may be the reason the relationship between you and your siblings is the way it is. It may be the reason you've come to treat your spouse a certain way. It may be the way you deal with the various rejections the world has given you. It may be in the way you relate to those within the church. It may be in how you treat your coworkers. It may be in the way you treat your children.

It may be found in the patterns of thought that consume you every day. It may be found in the ways you spend money and where you spend it. It may be found in the places you refuse to frequent, or the places you do frequent. It may be found in the apps on your phone, or the webpages in your history log. It may be found in your eating patterns, or even lack thereof. It may be found in how you spend your free time, or if you even allow yourself free time.

I don't know where you will find this in your life. One thing I've learned is that I've found it in my own life in more places than not, as if it is innately ingrained in our lives until we discover it.

If we can't recognize where this applies, we run the risk of living our lives on a hamster wheel. If we can't discover the root of the problem, we will spend our lives putting Band-Aids on wounds that need stitches. The root of the problem must be discovered in order to create long-lasting and genuine change.

We must often go backwards before we can step forward.

☙ ❧

This, I believe, is the harder of the two. This is more difficult than I care to presume. Sometimes we can't fathom why it would ever be worth it. Going backwards requires humility, honesty, vulnerability, and diligence. Often the process of going backwards is painful, while other times it is pain we are going back into. There is no universal one-size-fits-all process and what works for one person to "go backwards" is different for another. I do not write to tell you how to go back. Instead, I only write the following excerpts to show how going back brought me freedom, wisdom, and genuine change. My hope for doing this is so you may be encouraged to step into your own past and tackle those things which are keeping you from a real, true relationship with Jesus.

The Leaning Tower of Pisa is one of the most visited tourist attractions in Europe. Breaking ground in 1173 AD and built over the ensuing 200 years, the iconic bell tower stands roughly 56 meters tall today. Worth noting, the tower began leaning as soon as construction began as soft soils settled under the weight of the massive stones and marble.[2] Taken from the tower's official website, "the lean, first noted when three of the tower's eight stories had been built, resulted from the foundation stones being laid on soft ground consisting of clay, fine sand and shells."[3]

Engineers and architects tried to accommodate for the lean by building the inclined side taller than the opposite side. Their efforts resulted in the opposite effect: the weight of the taller walls on the sinking side caused the tower to lean even more.[4] The proposed solution made the matter worse, but construction was nonetheless completed.

In the twentieth century, as the tower inched its way closer to an emergency threshold, a team of engineers and architects was compiled to find a way to fix the gradually leaning tower. The ideas ranged from taking apart the tower stone-by-stone and rebuilding it somewhere else, installing concrete pillars into the foundation for stabilization, and adding concrete grout to the soils to stabilize it.[5]

In the end, engineers decided to drill holes into the ground opposite of the lean and remove soils in the hopes the tower would tilt back in the reverse direction. By attaching cables and pulling away from the lean, they slowly pulled the tower back against its lean, using the same method which

2. "Leaning Tower of Pisa," Leaning Tower of Pisa, 2018.
3. "Leaning Tower of Pisa," Historical Facts Page.
4. "Leaning Tower of Pisa," Historical Facts Page.
5. "Leaning Tower of Pisa," History Page.

caused the lean (soft and less soil) to remediate the lean. From breaking ground to finish, the process took over a decade and cost over 30 million Euro in 1990s' currency, which converted to today's USD is over $70 million.[6] They did not bring the tower back to perfect vertical, instead opting to bring it back within the safety zone of inclination and allowing the tower to continue to correct itself. Even today, the tower has continued to slowly right itself due to the work done by the engineers.

However, due to the nature of the soil on which the tower was built, projections and calculations show this correction will only be temporary before the tower comes to a standstill and then reverses course to lean once again.

Ultimately the tower will need to be corrected again. The only way to permanently correct the structure would be to disassemble the tower completely and rebuild it stone-by-stone on a solid foundation elsewhere.

Can you imagine?

A tower built nearly a millennia ago, where the best builders of the time tried various methods to correct the lean during the initial construction phase, where for generations and centuries since then people have sought to stabilize the tower, where finally a 10-year, multimillion-dollar-project was devised to fix it, only to discover the singular real solution would be to take the tower apart and build it elsewhere; to start over on the right foundation.

And this is what we must do.

Not unlike the Tower of Pisa, I built my life on a weak, soft foundation.

Growing up and having noticed areas where I lacked, I found myself trying and failing to alter my lean. My lean involved a toxic combination of inadequacy, rejection, drug and alcohol abuse, lust, addiction to pornography, selfishness, and pride.

A situation from my college years has held ramifications that I'm still working through today. After facing denial I found unable to bear, I remember committing myself to become the idyllic perfect man. In my mind, by becoming what I believed every woman wanted, I would never have to face and suffer rejection again.

This way my way of fixing the lean. I venture we've all had similar circumstances in our lives, where we attempt to make amends for our shortcomings. Where we pick up the remnants of something that's happened to

---

6. "Leaning Tower of Pisa," Historical Facts Page.

us and do our best to piece it back together. In my particular battle against rejection, I sought to become someone no one would reject.

Instead of being the guy who found himself crying over the grief of heartbreak, I wasn't going to be a sissy anymore. I learned to suppress any feelings resembling sadness, anger, or vulnerability. Those feelings which had gotten me into trouble before, I taught myself to bury deep down where eventually I couldn't even find them.

When I reflect on these happenings in my life, I can't help but notice these remedies for my faults resemble the manner the original engineers tried to correct the Tower of Pisa lean by building taller walls on the sinking side. All this did was make the burden heavier, the tower sinking and leaning even further. Similarly, my solutions only made my imminent fall much more perilous.

After being ridiculed by my friends for not being as sexually promiscuous as they were, I set out to prove my masculinity by joining in their wanton ways. Any thoughts of remorse or regret from these actions were drowned out through drinking. When the alcohol wasn't enough, I turned to Vyvanse and other amphetamines, marijuana, the party drug "molly," and psychedelic mushrooms. The deeper I delved into fixing my lean, the darker and more dangerous the tactics I tried.

Using my own tactics, I beat the lean of rejection I once felt. Instead of crying over girls, girls were crying over me. There was no more sadness or anger in my life anymore. Instead of allowing these feelings to surface, I'd consume more alcohol than I dare to recount and then go to the bars, only to wake up next to someone with no recollection of the night's events. I had proven to my friends that I had what it takes. I had proven I was more of a man now. I had it all: popularity, girls, friends, and fun. Nearly four years since I set out to become the ideal perfect man, I had achieved my goal. The man I envisioned was now looking back at me in the mirror.

Yet, and unsurprisingly, it was at this same time I found myself begging God every night to let me die because I had no hope and I no longer wanted to live.

"There is a way that appears to be right, but in the end it leads to death."[7]

It was on my bedroom floor on my knees between my bed and dresser where God met me. It was there he began to teach me the error of my ways and walk me backwards in order that I may step forward into what he's called for me.

7. Proverbs 14:12

In my experience of life up until this point, I believed my thoughts defined my reality. My thoughts of being a bad person, responsible for tragic events in peoples' lives, an imposter, fake, unworthy, deserving of pain and rejection—these must be true because I owned these thoughts. Therefore, I believed them to be true in the deepest depths of my being. As for those feeble moments when life became truly wearisome, those thoughts devolved into thinking I was a psychopath, mentally unstable, that I'd be better off dead, that life wasn't worth living, no one wanted me, and the only way out was taking my own life. These may seem trivial, as they appear irrational now, but these thoughts *defined* my experience for the first 24 years of life. The more anxiety-provoking the thought, the more I believed it to be true. In my mind, if it caused me to react in an anxious manner, then the underlying thought or fear must be true.

"As a man thinks in his heart, so he is."[8]

One of the first things God did was walk me through healing this thought pattern.

A visit to a Christian counselor for a perceived struggle with doubt turned into something much more with broader implications than I ever fathomed. Upon hearing the patterns of thought I used to process doubt regarding my faith, my counselor was wisely able to recognize something was abnormal. His prompting led to a trip to a psychiatrist for what he believed was a grander issue. After several visits with this psychiatrist and an antidepressant prescription, I was receiving therapy at the OCD Clinic of Louisville.

Obsessive Compulsive Disorder (OCD) is not what people think it is at all and this topic alone is another book on its own. To simplify OCD the best way I know how, it is a chronic disorder where the sufferer believes their worst thoughts and fears are true. One of my biggest fears was wanting to take my own life; therefore, my thoughts of potentially doing so caused so much anxiety that I believed this meant I must want to do it. My thoughts of being mentally unstable were so anxiety-provoking that I convinced myself it must be true. My thoughts of no one wanting me meant I believed just that: no one wanted me. There was no healing for these thoughts except for sleep, and these thoughts consumed my life for years. Sleeping became an escape of sorts, a peaceful oasis void of these thoughts.

---

8. Proverbs 23:7

Part I

There came a point when I couldn't see how things could possibly improve and my first thought in the morning became *"Oh no! I have to try to not kill myself today."*

It was a living hell. Anxiety and fear were my truth.

By God's grace, he walked me backwards through the trauma OCD caused me. One by one, day by day, we walked backwards through the lies I had believed my entire life. We did this through journaling and meditation. We did this through therapy and finally opening up about what was truly going on in my life to those around me. The more time I spent in prayer and his Word, the more truth was revealed to me, which counteracted my anxieties and fear.

The only way to describe my experience before this revelation was hopeless.

I knew hopelessness.

I did not understand how life could be worth what I was going through. However, in the quiet of time spent alone in relationship and the quiet of no social media, God walked me backwards through my trauma and pain and rebuilt the foundation on which I stood. From there he erected a new life for me, one rooted in truth and resting atop the cornerstone that is Jesus.

The process of going backwards brought confusion and sadness over my wasted years. That journey brought the pain that I needed to deal with to the surface; pain I had buried under the life I had built for myself. It required an honesty and vulnerability that shook the facade I created. Most importantly, I believe, it brought humility. Humility to understand the error of my ways. Humility to understand that I knew nothing about anything. Humility to submit to God's ways and allow his truth to shape my life.

It's been because I walked backwards that I am able to walk forward in a different manner than I would've believed possible. I've been able to walk into and through situations which would've once left me in panic. The doubts and anxieties still come, but because of what God allowed me to learn in going backwards, I'm able to confront them and they no longer cripple me to the extent they once did.

Even as I type these pages, I am amazed at how God has worked. My being here is nothing short of a miracle. I can see the picture of what he has done, and I glimpse what could be next. The humility my journey bestowed upon me rests at the forefront of this book. Humility has been a constant reminder that I am no different from the characters in the Bible.

From David the king to David the adulterer and murderer. From Job the blameless to Job the confused. From Peter the faithful to Peter the denier.

Through my walk backwards, I've been able to see I am no different from the Pharisees. Were I in their shoes 2,000 years ago, I would not have been able to recognize Jesus for who he was, yet Jesus loves me anyway and died for me nonetheless. It does not matter what we do, we can never make ourselves righteous in God's eyes. But no matter what we do, free grace through faith in Christ makes us righteous in God's eyes. It is a combination of these realizations which allows us to slowly recognize the Pharisee in ourselves and to turn, repent, and seek Jesus.

What God did for me (and will do for you) by taking me backwards in order to move forward is the only thing that could finally fix my (and your) lean. He took down the stones of my life one-by-one and rebuilt them on a solid foundation. This foundation does not waver and will not lean because it is a firm foundation.

When I reflect on human nature and think of how drastic it is to choose to walk backwards, I'm taken back by what I find. I would never have freely walked back had it not been something God orchestrated. I find the same to be true when it comes to fixing the Tower of Pisa. Even though engineers know the only true way to fix the tower is to take it apart and build elsewhere, they still resolve to merely tape it up and wait for another day. Another day when the timing feels right, or other things are in order.

I was no different. I am no different.

This process is not easy, but the rewards are worth it. Seeing Jesus is worth it. Experiencing the full life Jesus talks about in John 10 is worth it.[9]

The rest of this book is going to be about walking backwards to enable us to move forward. We will walk back to understand why the Pharisees acted in the manner they did when they saw Jesus. We will walk back to see how Jesus went unrecognized by those who devoted their lives to him. We will also walk backwards through parts of my life, which will hopefully encourage and empower you to do the same for yourself. We will walk back so we can see that the errors the Pharisees made are errors that are alive and active in our own lives. This will allow us to move forward without the same arrogance and blindness that caused the Pharisees to miss Jesus; and which we will likely find has inhibited many of us from recognizing Jesus in our

---

9. John 10:10 says, "The thief comes only to steal and kill and destroy; I have come that they may have life, and have it to the full."

own lives. The time for you is now, and I believe that the fact that you are reading this book is not a coincidence.

It's time to allow God to walk you backwards so you can move forward and recognize Jesus in areas he has long been missed by all of us.

4

Through Pride and Into Humility

<small>HUMILITY AND PRIDE.</small>

Pride and Humility.

In today's culture, the words are nearly synonymous with "good" and "bad," except they have become to mean the opposite of how they're portrayed in the Bible. The Bible teaches pride leads to destruction and is a sin. It teaches pride has no place in the body of Christ.

Humility, we are taught, leads to Christ for he boldly embodied humility. These are foundational truths we know and are taught. It's when we leave the walls of our Sunday school classes or bible-college that the reality of these words are revealed.

In today's culture, pride has culturally beneficial connotations. Pride is defined from Google's dictionary as "a feeling or deep pleasure or satisfaction derived from one's own achievements, the achievements of those with whom one is closely associated, or from qualities or possessions that are widely admired (noun)." An alternative definition reads "confidence and self-respect as expressed by members of a group, typically one that has been socially marginalized, on the basis of their shared identity, culture, and experience (noun)."[1]

As can be implied from the above definitions, we are taught to be proud of our work and who we are. We're taught to be proud of what we do and where we've come from. It's common to associate being proud with high self-confidence and an improved life experience.

---

1. Lexico Dictionaries, s.v. "pride."

Have you seen someone from your country cheer for another country's competitors during Olympic celebrations? What would you think of such an act? *Do you have no pride in where you come from?*

What do you find at the beginning or end of professional credentials for those who hold highly esteemed degrees? *Dr. Smith. John Smith, M.D. John Smith, P.E. John Smith, CCBA, etc.*

These abbreviations follow an English-language naming tradition where people adopt suffixes in order to display their accomplishments. During my MBA program, on several instances I was curtly instructed to use the Dr. suffix instead of Mr. or Mrs. or Ms. when calling a professor by name. These were clearly people who valued the esteem of pride in their position.

On the other end of the spectrum is humility, which is not far from the word humiliation. We're shown that humility looks a lot like not sticking up for ourselves and allowing ourselves to be bullied. It also looks like serving people, like a servant or slave. Humility means having little power and how many of us are taught being powerless is a good thing? How many of us are taught to pursue a life involving little to no power?

Not many.

We've grown up idolizing superheroes because they have special powers. We've grown up watching sports where power is on full display. We've grown up in a world ruled by power. A world where those with power rendezvous above the law; untouchable and indomitable. There are many things the world teaches us and one of those is the inherent credence that power is to be pursued.

In our world where pride and humility are identified as opposites, one can't be both proud and humble. Subsequently, we idealize proud as good and humility is thrown on the back burner.

The staff at *Bible Study Tools* lists Proverbs 3:5–6 in their *Top Ten Most Read Bible Verses* on their platform.[2] I can understand why as I repeat this verse to myself daily. In situations of doubt or anxiety or fear (or a combination of all three), these verses can be a refuge of hope. For years, when people asked my favorite bible verses, I would share these two with them.

However, little did I know that one of the biggest lessons in my faith would come from the very next verse.

---

2. "50 Most Popular & Favorite Bible Verses—Top Read Scripture Quotes," Bible Study Tools.

A few years ago I had a disastrous conversation with a close friend who had recently come out to me as being bisexual. I was new to the faith and arrogant when it came to what I believed. My newfound faith meant attending church on Sundays, no more wild partying until three in the morning, and using less foul language. Contrary to what I believed at the time, I was nowhere near ready to have the conversations I felt eager to dive into.

The story I'm about to share is one of those conversations. Remembering this story makes me sad for how wrong I was and for the implications our conversation had for him. I'm also incredibly grateful to have learned this lesson and recognized the error in my ways.

In a rare conversation about religion with this friend, he asked if I believed he was going to hell for being bisexual. Anticipating this conversation, I was eager to speak *my* truth into his life. I saw the opportunity as my chance and I jumped right into my rehearsed response.

I believed my new faith had given me the following wisdom: *"Being attracted to the same sex is not a sin, it's the practicing of it which is sinful. It's okay to have homosexual feelings and not act on them. However, as long as you practice and yield to those desires, I think it'll lead to hell."*

I'll never forget my friend's emotionally charged response.

"How could you believe that? My sin is the same as your sin."

Then he left.

I was both dumbfounded and at a loss for words. *Sorry the truth hurts sometimes,* I thought to myself.

I did not understand what he was talking about. How could he think our sins were the same? I had given up drinking. I had stopped practicing my own sexual innuendos. Drug use was a thing of the past. My sinful ways were behind me. In my mind, my sins weren't comparable to his sins—not even close!

How wrong I had been.

"Do not be wise in your own eyes; fear the LORD and shun evil."[3]

The wisdom in this verse had not yet been revealed to me. Even worse, I did not merely *think* I was wise and correct in my conviction, but I knew it. There wasn't a second thought about any error on my behalf for months after our conversation.

We often believe ourselves to be further in faith than our peers, thinking we know more because we have been a believer longer. In the case involving my friend (and which happens in church buildings across the

3. Proverbs 3:7

49

nation) I viewed myself as closer to God because I believed his sin was worse than mine. In actuality, *his sin was only more visible and culturally less-accepted than mine.*

(Hopefully that made the hair on the back of many necks stand up.)

This happens in our lives and churches every day. The sins of sexual immorality, stealing, adultery, drunkenness, addiction are much more visible than the sins of lust, pride, judgement, coveting, greed and envy. Too often, we take the ones who practice the former and name them as outcasts as we can easily identify their sins. What we get when this happens is a group of people who practice the latter, exiling those who practice the former. A broken system. A broken church.

Lucky for us, this is not a new problem. We've had this documented for us in the Bible: where clandestine sinners oppress and cast abuse upon the visible ones. By expanding on historians' ideals, we can apply lessons from the past and keep history from repeating itself.

Romans 3:10 reminds us *"There is not one who is righteous, not even one."*

If only we could truly understand and apply what this means. If only this was a verse written on our hearts and tattooed on our bodies. It is a reminder we are all equal, all sinners, and all equally detestable before God without Jesus.

A deeper understanding of this verse can help break down our pride. A deeper understanding of this verse can keep us from allowing history to repeat itself through our awareness of its relevance in issues today. To break down pride and move to a place of humility is essential to grasping all God has for you. Moving from pride into humility is essential to living the life God desires for you.

To begin breaking down pride, we need to understand how pride and humility are viewed in sight of God.

"When pride comes, then comes disgrace, but with humility comes wisdom."[4]

"The Lord detests all the proud of heart. Be sure of this: they will not go unpunished."[5]

"Haughty eyes and a proud heart—the unplowed field of the wicked—produce sin."[6]

---

4. Proverbs 11:2

5. Proverbs 16:5

6. Proverbs 21:4

"The proud and arrogant person—"Mocker" is his name—behaves with insolent fury."[7] [Insolent—showing a rude lack of respect[8]]

"Humility is the fear of the Lord; its wages are riches and honor and life."[9]

"Pride goes before destruction, a haughty spirit before a fall. Better to be lowly in spirit with the oppressed than to share plunder with the proud."[10]

What are these verses saying? That it's better to spend our time with outcasts? That it's to our benefit to spend time with downtrodden spirits? That humility will lead to a rich and honorable life? That disgrace comes from pride? That the Lord detests those who are proud of heart?

The verdict is clear—and the world has it flipped upside down and backwards—humility is to be sought and pride admonished. This is a radical lesson for the new believer, yet it's critically important to grasp.

Pride is hard to tackle because it is not seen and is merely a feeling. However, when unchecked, pride reaps destruction. For the Pharisees, unchecked pride led them to crucify the Son of the One True God from which their pride came from. Unchecked pride caused them to be blind when their God stood before them. Unchecked pride kept them from seeing where they may have been wrong when it came to God and his kingdom.

This unchecked pride is not resigned to the past and is present throughout our lives today. In order to grasp all this book has for you, it's critical to understand why pride needs to be left at the door—or in this case, the front cover of the book.

Before delving into Jesus' signature rebuke of the Pharisees in the seven woes, the following story, found in the book of Samuel, should be enough to humble even the most prideful among us.

The book of First Samuel recounts the history of Israel and surrounding territories during Israel's transition from being led by God to being led by a king.[11] During this time, the people of Israel voiced to the prophet Samuel their desire for an earthly king, just as their neighboring kingdoms had. They believed holding their heavenly God as sole king was not enough

7. Proverbs 21:24

8. Lexico Dictionaries, s.v. "insolent."

9. Proverbs 22:4

10. Proverbs 16:18–19

11. The Holy Bible, *New International Version*, *NIV*. Page 386. *Setting* note.

to protect and lead them. They didn't want an invisible being to lead them—in their minds, they needed a physical person.[12]

The Lord speaks to Samuel and advises him to seek and find the man he has chosen to lead Israel. This man is the son of Kish, Saul.[13] Samuel seeks out Saul and crowns him the king of the Israelites. In First Samuel 15:1–3, the prophet Samuel tells Saul the Lord wants him to "*attack the Amalekites and totally destroy all that belongs to them. Do not spare them; put to death men and women, children and infants, cattle and sheep, camels and donkeys.*"

The Amelekites had been butchering the Israelites since they crossed the Red Sea with Moses in Exodus. They were known to sporadically cross territorial borders and raid Israeli villages to the point where the people couldn't sleep in peace knowing what may happen during the night. In obedience to God's commands, Saul and his men attacked the Amalekites and destroyed their cities and towns.[14] They take their king, Agag, captive and kill the rest. As for the herds and livestock, they killed the sick and weak but *kept* the best of them for themselves.[15]

The explanation of the story should end here—the wicked are killed and the obedient are rewarded with riches. God's people are no longer in danger of being slaughtered and he has protected his people yet again. This should be yet another story of God's provision, similar to what's commonly found in the Old Testament.

In Judges 4, Barak and his army defeat the more powerful and better-equipped army of the Canaanites, giving Israel peace and riches through plunder.[16] The Lord delivered Gideon and his outnumbered army of 300 men to victory against the much greater Midianite army in Judges 7. Once again, in Joshua 6 the Israelites defeat the walled-city of Jericho and plunder its bronze and iron.[17]

However—unfortunately for Saul—there's a more delicate story this time.

---

12. 1 Samuel 8:5 says: *[The Israelites] said to [Samuel], "you are old, and your sons do not follow your ways; now appoint a king to lead us, such as all the other nations have.*

13. 1 Samuel 9:2.

14. 1 Samuel 15:7–8

15. 1 Samuel 15:9

16. Judges 5:30

17. Joshua 6:24

By putting context and cultural clues together, combined with piecing other parts of the story together, we can envision the story the way it may have unfolded all those years ago.

⤞ ⤝

The wind whips Saul's lengthy and greasy hair against the leathery, tough skin of his face. His dazzling bronze helmet rests firmly against his hip as he stands elevated before his men. The parched desert air is void except the faint metallic smell of blood, which pours from the defeated like the streams in the valley beyond. The Israeli army has just won a massive victory over another Amalekite city, and as such, the victors feel entitled to loot the city.

All city dwellings have been abandoned by their inhabitants in order to avoid the same fate as their lost soldiers. In that day and age, the citizens of a losing army have but two options: flee and try to find refuge or remain and face death or slavery. As such, the only movement in the dusty streets is the sputtering tap of goat hooves and other livestock as they explore their vacated surroundings. The deafening silence of a once-bustling city filled with trinkets and fortunes of those recently departed await the victorious soldiers.

The men stand before Saul, eagerly awaiting his victory speech before beginning their plunder. However, Saul's commands are unexpected. He orders them to destroy everything and leave nothing alive, following the commands God gave to Samuel. There are to be no slaves taken and no livestock kept alive in accordance with God's orders.

This is a first for the soldiers and contradicts the entire reason they came to fight: to plunder after a victory. Slaves hold significant value (as they always have throughout history). Women were sold as house or estate keepers. Children and young men made excellent and lifelong crop pickers and cheap laborers. Livestock held all sorts of value. They were used to work the land, served as sources for foor and milk, and produced value through breeding and trade.

The soldiers' wages are measly—but wealth came from plunder and was so desirable. These men risked their lives for it. In the ancient world, a victorious battle and successful plunder could transform societal class status. (Imagine playing the lottery but with your life and much better odds.)

Without the opportunity for plunder, most—or all—of the soldiers would have stayed home.

(Revoking the right to plunder would be similar to taking all of a waiter or waitress's tips and burning it all before them. *Ask a waiter or waitress if they would be willing to do their job without tips.*)

After hearing Samuel's instructions, it takes a few seconds for the soldiers to digest what they've heard before the army descends into chaos. A madhouse ensues as the livelihoods of the soldiers and their families is at stake.

High ranking officers request an emergency meeting to discuss what to do. Taking Saul into a makeshift command tent, they plead with Saul. "Sir this is outrageous! Our men are only here for this reason! If you do not allow them to plunder, they will never fight for you again!"

One man tells Saul what everyone else knows but is afraid to voice. "These men will riot and take our heads if we take this from them! We can either allow them to plunder or be killed!"

Panic begins to set in among the officers as they digest what they know all too well to be the truth. They may be skilled warriors, but the numbers are over a thousand-to-one against them. If the men revolt, as they are sure to do, there will be no survivors among them.

Another, more conniving member, gives his input. "What about this, Saul—we kill the weak ones but take the best ones with us and we will sacrifice them to the Lord. This way we all win. The Lord receives prized offerings and the soldiers don't revolt against you."

The men latch on to this as they perceive it as their only way out alive.

Saul contemplates the conundrum while yet another officer reasons with him. "Yes, Saul, this is what you must do. Surely the Lord would rather receive offerings than for us to slaughter all the livestock. What good does that do anyone? After all, the Lord never spoke to us, merely Samuel, and he's not a warrior like us so he doesn't understand the importance of the matter. He surely didn't mean to kill *everything*! It was clearly just a mix-up of words."

Lastly, a certain, yet unspoken option remains among Saul's officials— the officers could kill Saul and inform the soldiers Saul changed his mind and decided to allow them to loot. The army would never know what really happened. Nor would they likely have cared.

∽ ∾

Removing ourselves from the story, we can discern that Saul had two options:

1. order the men to kill everything and risk certain death or rebellion by his men or

2. allow the sick and weak to be killed and the best kept to be offered to the Lord as sacrifices.

By agreeing to the second option, Saul gets to keep his life and appease Samuel, his soldiers, his officers, and his God—at least this is what Saul believes.

I don't know about you, but I know which option I'd take in Saul's shoes. Saul is fundamentally choosing to live or die. Unsurprisingly, he chooses his life, and he tries to convince himself it's what the Lord wants of him. The weak and sick animals are killed by his men, and the healthy and strong are kept. As for the enemy combatants, we are told they are all killed except for their king, Agag.

The only reason we are given for why Agag is allowed to live because he was "good."[18] This is not to be interpreted as he was a good person, but rather he was useful—similar to how the healthy livestock was kept while the weak and sick were killed. To control one's king was to control one's kingdom. As long as they held Agag captive, they had control over other Amalekite territories. Thus, by keeping Agag they were ensuring they had control and power over his people.

Away from the action, the Lord appears to Samuel and informs him Saul did not obey his commands in their entirety.[19] For this disobedience, the Lord proclaims he regrets ever making Saul king and he will choose another to lead his people.

Samuel is furious at Saul.

When Samuel confronts Saul about his disobedience, Saul, in typical human fashion, swiftly points out the areas where he did follow the Lord's instruction and conquered the Amalekites.

"When Samuel reached him, Saul said "The Lord bless you! I have carried out the Lord's instructions."[20]

Saul rushes to speak first so he can point out his obedience.

Samuel, however, gets straight to the point, asking *"what then is this bleating of sheep in my ears? What is this lowing of cattle that I hear?"*[21]

18. 1 Samuel 15:9
19. 1 Samuel 15:11
20. 1 Samuel 15:13
21. 1 Samuel 15:14

In other words, Samuel is saying, "*I didn't come here to discuss how you were obedient. I came here because you were disobedient.*"

Saul, still wanting to believe he's in the right, responds how I would.

"*Saul answered, 'The soldiers brought them from the Amalekites; they spared the best of the sheep and cattle to sacrifice to the Lord your God, but we totally destroyed the rest.'*"[22]

Saul blames the soldiers. *It's not his responsibility for their actions*, he insinuates to himself and to Samuel.

Saul also tries to sweet-talk Samuel, telling him they only kept the best to sacrifice to Samuel's God. To further make his point, Saul again reminds Samuel where he followed the instructions, by "*totally*" destroying the rest.

It's hard to imagine how we can possibly relate to this now; it's the twenty-first century and none of us have plundered for a living.

Nevertheless, look at this sentence from Saul (verse 15)! It's always someone else's fault and not our own—and then don't forget the cherry on top, "I totally did what you asked of me."

Humans are so predictable.

I believe Saul knew his decision was wrong. Others will disagree. They will claim Saul was truly doing what he believed the Lord wanted of him. This makes sense—why else would the Lord want the Amelekites destroyed other than to reward the Israelites, God's own people? Why would the Lord not allow them to be blessed through plunder? Why would the Lord not want their prized offerings, the best of what was available? The Lord had done this before for his armies, and these are all justifiable points.

Saul made the same choice I would have made—the choice most of us would have made. He chose his own life over complete obedience to the Lord. He chose convenience over commitment.

Saul chose what made sense in this world, rather than follow what God commanded.

It is my belief that deep down, Saul knew he made a mistake. He knew he had been caught in disobedience even though he was obedient in most of what the Lord had asked of him. Yet, by not being completely obedient, he was being wholly disobedient.

Pastor Michael Todd of Transformation Church, in *Who's the Minister Here: Bandwagon Believers*, explains this further when he refers to even slow obedience as disobedience.[23] James, the half-brother of Jesus, also

22. 1 Samuel 15:15
23. Todd, Michael. "Bandwagon Believer." *Who's The Minister Here?*

writes *"For whoever keeps the whole law and yet stumbles at just one point is guilty of breaking all of it."*[24]

When you do only some of what God asks, rather than being fully obedient, you are being disobedient.

Several verses later Saul reveals the reason for his disobedience, and it illuminates the basis of this particular retelling of the story you've found yourself reading.

"I was afraid of the men and so I gave into them."[25]

The truth comes out. Saul can't take it anymore as he's overwhelmed by the guilt and shame he's tried to reason away. He attempted to stand strong in obedience to the Lord's instructions, but eventually his fear of the soldiers—and fear of losing his life—outweighs his fear of the Lord.

Who wouldn't have made the same decision as Saul?

It appears to be common sense. There were 200,000 armed men against the invisible God of Samuel. Saul would have risked his life to fully obey the Lord's commands. If he had ordered all livestock killed, it was far more likely the soldiers would have killed him and kept the livestock anyway. He was hopeless, and so he gave in.

Now he falls to Samuel's feet.

"I beg you, forgive my sin and come back with me, so that I may worship the Lord."[26]

Unfortunately for Saul, the Lord has already decided, and Saul has been rejected. Samuel and the Lord leave Saul, never to return to him again.

❧　❧

What is the point of this story?

If anything, it should scare us because Saul's blip of disobedience causes the Lord to reject him for good. Saul was obedient 99 percent of the time, but the one time he wasn't he paid the ultimate price.

What might this look like today? How could we possibly relate to this story?

It may look like going to church every week, tithing, volunteering, sponsoring children, and constantly serving the poor and needy, sharing the gospel as you go. Then, after a long day of service to the Lord, you look at that page on your phone that you shouldn't. You wish you had something

24. James 2:10
25. 1 Samuel 15:24
26. 1 Samuel 15:25

your next-door neighbor has. You think enviously about your friend in that seemingly perfect relationship while you lay down alone. You fall asleep angry with your partner instead of working it out.

BAM!

Just like that, the Lord leaves you, and no amount of repenting or begging will bring him back!

Thankfully—and that's not the correct word that should be used here—this is not what happens to us. Because of what Jesus did for us, when we ask for forgiveness—no matter what we do—we receive it. Sure, there will be consequences derived from our sin, but when God sees us, he only sees our goodness. Jesus took what we deserved to the cross with him and let it kill him. He suffocated for hours on his own blood because he knew we could never be enough for God. His love for us and desire to be united with us cost Jesus his life.

I can't even pretend I'm obedient 99 percent of the time like Saul was. Most days I don't feel like I'm even a mere 10 percent obedient. It's because of this that we must understand pride has no place in our lives. When we want to point others to the things we do right, we need to instead be pointed to things they do right. No matter what we do, we are detestable before God without Jesus. And Jesus didn't come to us because of the good we've done either. He came while we were still sinners.[27]

Moving past pride and into humility is difficult and requires constant diligence. Many steps forward can be quickly backtracked by becoming unaware of that which we've discussed, how pride must have no home in us. While it's empowering to celebrate progress in this respect, becoming complacent in seeking humility will quickly allow pride to sneak back in and reverse any progress.

This is partly what makes pride so difficult to overcome—it must constantly be at the forefront of our thoughts so we can continue to walk in grace and remember that it's only through grace by which we live and breathe.

As you discovered in the Prologue and will continue to see throughout this work, I've been challenged by the intensity of this realization many times during the writing of these words. It is simply too easy to be caught up in prideful living and thinking. It will appear in your life like a thief in the night before you have any idea what's going on. It's too easy to seek

27. Romans 5:8

glory for ourselves in miniscule, almost indistinct, ways. However, we all do it. It's part of our nature. It's part of being human.

As we finally begin our dive into Jesus' most notable rebuke of the Pharisees in the seven woes, you will be reconciled with the weight of who the Pharisees were—people like you and me.

In many respects, they were better than us. By understanding this, we may have a chance at keeping history from repeating itself. By identifying with the Pharisees, we can see Jesus more clearly in our everyday lives. If and when this happens, other peoples' lives will be changed along with our own.

Buckle up because the woes are about to come to life.

PART II

5

The First Woe

"Woe to you, teachers of the law and Pharisees, you hypocrites! You shut the door of the kingdom of heaven in people's faces. You yourselves do not enter, nor will you let those enter who are trying to. [They devour widows' houses and for a show make lengthy prayers. These men will be punished most severely.]"

MATTHEW 23:13–14 (verse 14 is really Mark 12:40 and Luke 20:47)

TODAY, IT'S OVERTLY COMMON to approach this verse—and the entirety of this extensive seven-part rebuke—from the viewpoint of Jesus exposing the schemes of the religious leaders.

Following this perspective, the Pharisees were merely puppeteers. They knew the real way to heaven, but purposefully chose to follow a different path and did their best to trick others into joining them. This perspective would mean their objective was to get to hell and take many people with them. Jesus, in his white robe and with his effortlessly windblown mane of hair, has once again come to the rescue of the poor and oppressed by calling out the tricksters who are purposely leading people away from God.

ᴄ∾ ∾ᴄ

This could not be further from the reality of the time.

The Talmud (quick reminder: written compilation of the long-debated and dissected Oral Law) contains hundreds and hundreds of discussions and philosophical debates between the Pharisees. I urge you to take a look for yourself at the Talmud, but you can rest assured from my understanding and numerous studies these were some of the greatest intellectual minds of their time. Their ability to call to mind Scripture and apply its teachings to all facets of life is truly remarkable. Their brains operated like computers in that they were able to see or hear a situation and immediately mentally scan and sort through thousands of pages of texts to find the solution as it related to the written and oral law. In my opinion there is nothing remotely comparable in today's world to their complete devotion and extraordinary memorization.

When Jesus was just a boy, he spent three days after the Jewish festival of Passover in Jerusalem in the temple courts listening to the Pharisees' teachings and asking them questions.[1] I have been a 12-year-old boy before and there was nothing in the world interesting enough to keep my attention for three days. Likewise, Jesus was drawn to simply sit among the teachers and hear their wisdom and to increase his own understanding. He knew his parents would be worried sick when they couldn't find him, but it was more important for Jesus to be there, learning in his Father's house from the wisest men in Judaism. They had much to teach Jesus.

Doesn't this story contradict the relationship we've grown to believe existed between Jesus and the Pharisees and other religious leaders? Twelve-year-old Jesus was not rebuking and calling to attention the hypo-critical incorrectness of the Pharisees. Rather he was sitting among them and learning from them.[2]

If Jesus is God and he understood their wisdom and needed to learn from them, *maybe we do too.*

These men had committed their entire lives to serving the Jewish God by keeping the Laws of Moses. They debated its instructions relating to cultural and societal values and obeyed and debated and obeyed and debated some more. Each law was applied to every facet of their life. Years upon years upon their lifetimes were spent studying and applying Jewish laws.

We think we may be giving up too much when the church asks for 10 percent of our income, or a night each week for groups, or a few hours of volunteering each month, or 10 minutes of daily prayer, or some other facet beyond our own agenda; but nothing we do can compare to what the ancient Pharisees sacrificed for their God.

1. Luke 2:42–47
2. Luke 2:46

If any of the Jewish people understood God and how to get closer to him, it was these men. Jonathan David from Bethel refers to the Pharisees as worship leaders, professional worshippers, and leaders of the church during the day.[3] Separating Pharisees from other religious leaders was the notion that they didn't keep their practices and knowledge to themselves, but instead used their wisdom and zeal to show other Jews how to live a life that would allow them to understand and know God. Because of the Pharisees, more Jews than ever were living a life of worship to God. They lived a complete life of dedication.

Which means in this first woe, Jesus wasn't simply exposing purposeful false motives as we may have originally believed. Jesus was essentially telling them, "Everything you think you are doing right, you are wrong."

Needless to say, this did not sit well with the Pharisees.

Why would it?

How do we handle being told we are wrong? Especially when it's something we are confident we are correct in? Particularly when it's in areas where we believe God has asked for our obedience and we have obeyed? How would we handle being told this by someone we trust? Imagine being told this by someone who posed a threat to us (as Jesus posed a threat to them).

First: *Who does this poor carpenter think he is?*

Second: *How dare he criticize our life's work. How dare he try to turn this on us.*

Third: *What man thinks he can question what God has called us to?*

As it was, the first woe Jesus released upon the Pharisees charged them with doing the opposite of what they thought they were doing.

They didn't think they were shutting the door to the kingdom in peoples' faces, and they certainly didn't think they themselves weren't entering that kingdom. It can be nearly assured that this was the last thing they believed to be true about their work and lives.

They were respected and popular religious leaders because of their progressiveness. They undoubtedly opened more doors to the kingdom than the Sadducees and other Jewish sects. More Jews were living a life devoted to God than ever before (as described in Chapter 1). Because of this, and due to how many people they taught to follow the One God, certainly they themselves were going to enter the heavenly kingdom.

Still, Jesus turns these certainties on a dime.

3. Jonathan David and Melissa Helser, "The Kind of Worship God Desires."

Part II

It is the first woe of seven that will all but surely seal his fate.

What was Jesus talking about in this woe? What does it look like to shut the door to the kingdom in peoples' faces and not enter ourselves?

To help you envision what this looks like, I'm going to give an example of how I've seen this play out in my life as well as how this played out during Jesus' time. It's critically important to understand what this looked like in ancient times, but also to show how radically different, yet similar, I've seen this play out in my own life.

∽ ∾

Today, if someone walked down the street in torn clothes, covering half their face and screaming "Unclean! Unclean!" I would believe that person insane.

However, in the ancient world, this was a common occurrence. Moses writes in Leviticus that this is what people must do if deemed unclean. It was critically important that diseases were prevented from spreading amongst the population.[4] As such, someone carrying a disease or ailment had to be separated from society and flagged as unclean.

"Anyone with such a defiling disease must wear torn clothes, let their hair be unkempt, cover the lower part of their face and cry out, 'Unclean! Unclean!' 46 As long as they have the disease, they remain unclean. They must live alone; they must live outside the camp."[5]

This rule was to make sure everyone knew an unclean person was coming near so they could stay away to avoid accidentally becoming unclean themselves. As I will discuss later, the process of becoming clean after being deemed unclean is incredibly delicate and time consuming. Ideally, one would do this as few times per day as possible in order to spend more time with God. In essence, don't be unclean, but rather clean and pure before a clean and pure God.[6]

4. When I began writing this book in early 2019, Covid-19 had not yet turned the world upside down. It would be another year before the spread of this disease brought the US near standstill. However, these words were written before their implications would be part of the everyday conversation.

5. Leviticus 13:45–46

6. Leviticus 11:44–45 says, "I am the Lord your God; consecrate yourselves and be holy, because I am holy. Do not make yourselves unclean by any creature that moves along the ground. 45 I am the Lord, who brought you up out of Egypt to be your God; therefore be holy, because I am holy." Leviticus 19:2 says, ""Speak to the entire assembly of Israel and say to them: 'Be holy because I, the Lord your God, am holy." Leviticus 20:26

Do whatever you have to do to stay clean[7]—this is the heart of the purity code.

Now let's follow up the laws found in Leviticus 13 with instructions in Leviticus 26:14–22.

> [14]*"But if you will not listen to me and carry out all these commands,* [15]*and if you reject my decrees and abhor my laws and fail to carry out all my commands and so violate my covenant,* [16]*then I will do this to you: I will bring on you sudden terror, wasting diseases and fever that will destroy your sight and sap your strength. You will plant seed in vain, because your enemies will eat it.* [17]*I will set my face against you so that you will be defeated by your enemies; those who hate you will rule over you, and you will flee even when no one is pursuing you.*
>
> [18]*"If after all this you will not listen to me, I will punish you for your sins seven times over.* [19]*I will break down your stubborn pride and make the sky above you like iron and the ground beneath you like bronze.* [20]*Your strength will be spent in vain, because your soil will not yield its crops, nor will the trees of your land yield their fruit.*
>
> [21]*"If you remain hostile toward me and refuse to listen to me, I will multiply your afflictions seven times over, as your sins deserve.* [22]*I will send wild animals against you, and they will rob you of your children, destroy your cattle and make you so few in number that your roads will be deserted."*

Woah . . .

These are the Lord's words. These are the thing's God told the Israelites would happen to them if they did not obey ALL of his decrees and commands.

They would be subject to terror and disease.

They would go hungry and be enslaved by their enemies.

Lastly, they as a people would be decimated.

I have not been blessed with children yet, however, it is something I constantly pray and hope for. One day, God willing, if I have children, they will be my greatest joy and biggest love. I've heard it's a love I can't even fathom and that excites me more than words can express.

---

says, "You are to be holy to me because I, the Lord, am holy, and I have set you apart from the nations to be my own."

7. In Leviticus 15:31, the Lord instructs Moses, "'You must keep the Israelites separate from things that make them unclean, so they will not die in their uncleanness for defiling my dwelling place, which is among them.'"

One of the worst things I can fathom would be to have a wild animal take my child from me. (See verse 22.)

I am athletic and well-built. Nevertheless, a cat could rip my skin to shreds. I'm talking about measly little house pets, not the bigger ones. There are wild animals out there I will be just fine never seeing in my life. I'm a human and have a brain for a reason—fighting animals would've left us extinct.

Point in case, I would do everything possible to ensure I didn't disobey God's commands so he wouldn't send a tiger to eat my children. I know this sounds absurd in our day and age; but this was not the case 2,000 years ago. Lions roamed freely, as did elephants, cheetahs, and anacondas and vipers. This would have been a very real and frightening threat. After all, it was coming from God who has the power to do as he pleases. Because of this, I would make sure I had the previous rules and teachings of Leviticus read and memorized upside down, diagonal, and backwards.

You say you bumped your head against the door? Uh-huh . . . come here!

That looks thicker than skin to me! Maybe I'm being too hasty, but I think I see a single yellow hair too, not sure because I'm not getting close anymore. You must go to the priest! Jeez! You're unclean! Get out! Get out! Get OUT! UNCLEAN! UNCLEAN!

Now this would merely be my reaction to Leviticus 13:29–30.[8] There are over a dozen chapters and hundreds of rules throughout the book of Leviticus that would inspire a similar reaction in me.

The book of Leviticus is not alone in this regard, either. Beginning in Exodus 21 and extending through chapter 30, God presents dozens more laws to Moses and the Israelites to follow and promises severe punishments if they aren't obeyed. In Leviticus 10, Aaron's sons Nadab and Abihu offer an *unauthorized* fire before the Lord—"unauthorized" because they didn't precisely follow the Lord's instructions for offerings. In response to not following his commands precisely, *"fire came out from the Lord's presence and consumed them,"* killing them instantly.[9]

My point is this—when the Pharisees avoided lepers and made sure they were societal outcasts, they were merely being obedient to God. They

---

8. Leviticus 13:29–30 says, "If a man or woman has a sore on their head or chin, the priest is to examine the sore, and if it appears to be more than skin deep and the hair in it is yellow and thin, the priest shall pronounce them unclean; it is a defiling skin disease on the head or chin."

9. Leviticus 10:2

took God at his word and did exactly what he told them to do so they wouldn't have to face his wrath.

Then, God himself came down and did seemingly the opposite when it came to lepers and others who were unclean. Then, he chastised the Pharisees for their actions which appeared to be obeying him. The Pharisees were only keeping those people at a distance as God commanded them. Yet when Jesus stood before them, he proposes that this distancing effectively shut the door to the kingdom.

What? Is God confused? Don't you remember what you said before?

Could this happen today? How does this happen in our own lives? How do we live a life where we avoid falling into a similar cycle?

On social media a while ago, I saw a friend of mine post the following ad for a roommate. It went along the lines of this: "*Seeking a roommate! Any female and CHRISTIAN who is interested please message me!*"

This made sense to me.

After all, Proverbs 13:20 says "*Whoever walks with the wise becomes wise, but the companion of fools will suffer harm.*"

Second Corinthians 6:14–15 reads, "*Do not be unequally yoked with unbelievers. For what partnership has righteousness with lawlessness? Or what fellowship has light with darkness? What accord has Christ with Belial? Or what portion does a believer share with an unbeliever? What agreement has the temple of God with idols?*"

We can't forget about Psalm 1:1–4: "*Blessed is the man who walks not in the counsel of the wicked, nor stands in the way of sinners, nor sits in the seat of scoffers; but his delight is in the law of the Lord, and on his law he meditates day and night. He is like a tree planted by streams of water that yields its fruit in its season, and its leaf does not wither. In all that he does, he prospers. The wicked are not so, but are like chaff that the wind drives away.*"

I believe it was out of obedience to what the Bible teaches that my friend sought a Christian roommate in order to grow and mature as a believer.

In many ways, I agree with her perspective. I have been on the opposite side of this situation and lived with unbelievers while trying to grow and mature in my relationship with Jesus. I will be the first to tell you that it caused many setbacks. It was too easy for my roommate to pass a marijuana pen across the room and for me to indulge when I knew it was something I shouldn't be doing. It was too easy to drink when my roommates had friends over before going out to the bars. It was too easy to follow along with gossip while relaxing and watching a movie. It was too easy to watch the movie scene I shouldn't have watched when hanging with my roommates.

I was exposed to sin constantly that affected me in ways I was both aware and unaware of.

I believe living with like-minded believers would have been beneficial and would have drastically reduced the temptations that I faced. Therefore, these Bible verses make sense and I can validate them as true. Extrapolating their meanings into real life situations, I can see why my friend's ad sought a Christian roommate.

However, there is a flip side to this argument. For someone on the outside of the Christian faith, this ad appears noticeably exclusive. The church has a bad reputation in this regard, especially in today's culture where sexuality and abortion are political hot topics. If an unbeliever saw this ad, they would be even further turned away from the idea of religion.

By living with only fellow believers, we are missing out on intimate relationships with unbelievers. I cannot read minds, and therefore I try not to pretend I know what is going on in others' thoughts. However, for each time I took the marijuana pen from my roommate, there were another five times I turned it down to remain sober. For each time I would drink with their friends, there were 10 times where I would remain sober even as I continued to hang out with them. For each time I gave into gossiping, there were other times where I refused to gossip. For every inappropriate movie scene I watched, there was another movie I refused to watch to avoid temptation.

I am not ignorant enough to believe that each time I chose the narrow path I was noticed by others. I am also not arrogant enough to believe my decisions necessarily made a positive impression on unbelievers who were there to witness.

However, I worship an enormous God and I know the significance his power can behold in a single moment. I've witnessed God use a seemingly obscure moment to dramatically shift the course of my life.

I would venture to believe the same has happened in your life.

The way God used me led to my brother's baptism. The countless discussions I had with my roommates and roommates' friends about life and faith could have had an impact on their lives of which I am wholly unaware. For every time I fell into temptation or sin, there may have been equal opportunities where I showed Jesus to someone in a way they never experienced.

"He also said, "This is what the kingdom of God is like. A man scatters seed on the ground. [27]Night and day, whether he sleeps or gets up, the seed sprouts and grows, though he does not know how. [28]All by itself the soil produces grain—first the stalk, then the head, then the full kernel in the head. [29]As soon as the grain is ripe, he puts the sickle to it, because the harvest has come."[10]

We simply don't know and cannot underestimate the power in a moment's interaction with an unbeliever. Our God has done greater things than we can fathom.

When Jesus touched the leper, the Pharisees saw him disobeying God's commands. Leviticus 7:21 told them anyone who becomes unclean must be cut off from other people—yet this man who had claimed deity just touched someone unclean.[11] (Remember the other Leviticus verse which reiterated this by saying the Israelites must stay separated from unclean things so they don't die.[12])

You can probably imagine and understand how the confusion we experience today is no different from the confusion the Pharisees experienced when Jesus came along with teachings which they believed antagonized God's laws. We are going to continue to find similar predicaments between Jesus and the Jewish leaders which, once broken down, will resemble many challenges we are faced with today.

Moving on.

Part of my story as I became a believer was the radical shift from alcohol and drug abuse. Starting at 16-years-old and continuing to evolve over the next eight years, my life revolved around the party scene and all it entailed. As such, my friends were all caught up in the same and following the same errant path.

The first move I made when surrendering my life to Christ was to give up everything involved in the party scene. I gave up consumption of alcohol and drugs and severed ties with anyone who still practiced the partying way of life.

I filled my time with everything I came to believe God was asking me to do. I began volunteering with a local young adult ministry at church

---

10. Mark 4:26–29

11. Matthew 8:3

12. Leviticus 15:31 says, "'You must keep the Israelites separate from things that make them unclean, so they will not die in their uncleanness for defiling my dwelling place, which is among them.'"

and leading as many groups as I could fit into my schedule. When I wasn't volunteering, I spent time getting to know my new believing friends. By spending all my time surrounded by God and his people, I didn't have time to fall into the temptation that was readily awaiting me from my old life. My new life had become devoid of those things and people which had traversed life with me for so long.

Looking back, however, I can see clearly how I was shutting the door to the kingdom in peoples' faces.

I had been a part of the party scene long enough to know my departure would've been discussed among my abandoned acquaintances. I, myself, had been one of the first to ridicule someone who left the party scene for their faith. I surely would have been the punch line of jokes for many people.

Furthermore, I did not invite anyone along with me in my new walk with Christ. I walked out the door and shut it behind me.

By spending all my time with new believing friends, I found I was giving up a lot of time previously spent with my family. Where I used to go home on Sundays and hang out with my parents and younger sister, I now spent this time doing things I was fully convinced God was asking me to do—like volunteering in ministry and building a new community of believers.

Even further convincing me of the need to do these things was God's own Word.

"If anyone comes to me and does not hate father and mother, wife and children, brothers and sisters—yes, even their own life—such a person cannot be my disciple."[13]

While I clearly did not come to hate my family, I nevertheless used this verse to justify the noticeable distance growing between my family and myself. This distance continued to grow and culminated in my decision to skip a family vacation to Jamaica with the excuse of not being able to get off work. In truth, I never even asked my employer if it would be allowed. Even more, I haven't worked for the company since early 2018 and it wouldn't have mattered in the long run anyways.

Breaking my heart even further, my family did not condemn me during these times. Instead, they loved me from a distance as they were happy I finally seemed to possess a joy that had long averted me.

13. Luke 14:26

Eventually—and while I understand this isn't my doing, I believe my absence played a factor—my family really started hurting in multiple areas. My parents' 30-year marriage struggled as empty nest syndrome took its hold on them. The tension was obvious and I sought to avoid this negative atmosphere by spending even more time away from home.

Then, my younger sister began struggling with mental health. Having gone through my own battle with this, I should've been there for her—but I wasn't. Before I knew it, she was in an inpatient recovery center for people struggling with self-harm and suicidal tendencies. My beautiful and vibrant baby sister was losing her battle with those same demons only Jesus could've saved me from and I was at church instead of sharing the gospel with her.

At the time this was occurring, I could not see where I was wrong. Only my ability to identify with the Pharisees has allowed me to see backwards into my faults during this time. Using God's word, I was doing what I believed he asked me to do in being distant from my family. My deep convictions told me something was wrong, but it was easier to be surrounded by the positive atmosphere I found at church and in a new community than to face the demons that appeared to take over my family life.

Aside from my family, my old friends were left in the dust too. Using the same verses described in detail above, I turned my back on them and didn't look back. I didn't invite them into what I was doing and I neglected any invitation to join them in their debauchery. Slowly but surely, these relationships began to crumble and were lost. While many of these relationships needed to be lost, some of the people I left behind are and were very good people; better than myself. The only reason I believed I had to abandon them was simply because they weren't followers of Jesus.

As can be blatantly evident today, sometimes unbelievers make better people than those who claim to believe in God.

Even though I felt strong convictions about and against the way I abandoned them, I used my understanding of God's Word to keep pushing forward the path I was convinced God was calling me down. This path seemed clear—only Jesus and those who know him. Looking at it this way, my path no longer included my family and former friends.

I carried on like this for months until one day, in a coffee shop, God revealed his truth to me in a way I could no longer ignore.

"I desire mercy, not sacrifice."[14]

14. Matthew 9:13. Hosea 6:6.

Jesus says these words to his disciples. He also tells the Pharisees to go and learn what this means.

In this particular moment, Jesus spoke it into my soul.

He was telling me in the same manner he told the Pharisees—Everything you think you are doing right, you are wrong.

I had been living my Christian life as if it was a game of who could sacrifice the most. *Look at me . . . I gave up my family and friends and they're struggling but I'm still standing strong. I also gave up drinking and using drugs. I had sacrificed the most.*

My view of what God asked of me was flawed. Making it even more confusing and easier to ignore was that I appeared to be following God's commands. I was distanced from my family and no longer yoked to unbelievers, just as God calls us to do. Right?

Wrong.

"To do what is right and just is more acceptable to the Lord than sacrifice." Proverbs 21:3

Sadly, it took me so long, too long, to realize this. Thankfully, God wrecked my soul in a way I couldn't fathom when he exposed his Word in the coffee shop through 5 words.

It hit me hard.

It still hits me now!

Not only had I been shutting the door to the Kingdom of Heaven in peoples' faces, but I can clearly see now how I, myself, wasn't going to enter either.

This is exactly what Jesus charged the Pharisees with doing in the first woe.

I wasn't inviting people into this new life God blessed me with. Instead, I was doing the opposite and avoiding those who weren't believers. I was sacrificing those relationships instead of showing mercy.

The Pharisees were doing the same thing. They were using God's word to distance themselves from those deemed unclean and who didn't believe in the same way.

While they were confidently lost in what they believed to be their unmatched devotion and obedience to God, Jesus informed them that they were actually being disobedient.

The following stories and interactions highlight the many times Jesus showed what God's word meant as opposed to how it was being used.

Understand how radical they must've been to be written down for the world to know.

When Jesus comes down from the mountainside in Matthew 8:1 after the Sermon on the Mount, a leper screaming *"Unclean! Unclean!"* made his way to Jesus.[15] The crowds must have parted like the Red Sea with Moses when the man wearing shredded clothes and the unforgettable cloth on his face approached them. The Pharisees were furthest from the leper—the professed cleanest people present.

Instead of running away, Jesus pivots and allows the man to approach him. Then, in an act so extraordinary to Jesus' generation, he reaches out and touches the leper.

When the Samaritan woman in John 4 approaches the well where Jesus is resting while his disciples fetch lunch, the woman expects to be ignored as she is an outcast and known sinner. Those who know God's laws obey his commands and stay away from her. This is how all religious people have interacted with her since her wayward life became public—*they don't.*

Instead of ignoring her, Jesus asks her for water. She is completely shocked. Jesus proceeds to tell her he knows everything about her life[16] and that he is the Messiah.[17] Many Samaritans would soon become believers because of this single interaction.

Then there's what happened to Levi (Matthew) the tax collector as he sat in his booth. He expected Jesus and those with him to keep walking by, for he was a tax collector, hated by the Jews for cheating them and becoming rich through lies and deceit.[18]

Instead of walking by, Jesus invites him to follow him.

The same thing happens to a tax collector known as Zacchaeus. He climbs a sycamore-fig tree to get a look at Jesus, knowing no one would dare help him see over the crowd.[19] Zacchaeus is expecting to be ignored as Jesus passes by.

Jesus instead calls him down to have dinner at his home.

Further, when the prostitute in Luke 7 approaches Jesus at the Pharisee's house, she is expected to be thrown out and ridiculed—for she is a

---

15. Matthew 8:2. While this verse does not tell us the leper's words, Jewish law and customs required him to repeat these words.

16. John 4:39

17. John 4:26

18. Matthew 9:9.

19. Luke 19:3–4

prostitute and an uninvited guest in the house of a religious leader. She is unclean and should not be touched.[20]

Instead of throwing her out, Jesus allows her to wash his feet. In another act so uncustomary and downright blasphemous to the Pharisees, Jesus forgives her sins.[21]

When the woman caught in adultery is brought to Jesus in the temple courts, she expects to die,[22] for God told Moses anyone caught in adultery is to be stoned to death.[23] In obedience to God's law, she should be killed.

Instead of condemning her to die, Jesus writes on the ground. He doesn't condemn her, and he reminds the foolish crowd—most of whom by now are long gone—they have no right to condemn her either.

Pay close attention to what Jesus truly did here.

He accepted those who made a living through cheating and deceit. He forgave and cleansed those who God originally instructed Moses to stone to death. He acknowledged those who had been blatantly disobedient to God's laws. He touched those who had been instructed to be outcasts and avoided.

We can't afford to miss this.

Our God is a God who uses uncustomary, un-cultural, and socially unacceptable interactions to do the extraordinary. Our God is above the law and he has no rules to follow. He is justice, righteousness, and truth. Therefore, so is Jesus.

Because of this, our walk with Jesus will have to lead us past the law and into situations where others would be shocked and offended. When you find yourself here, you will know that Jesus is with you. When you find yourself here, you will know the heart of God.

Do not fall into the same trap as the Pharisees and shut the door to the Kingdom of Heaven in people's faces. Do not fall into the same trap I fell into when I shut the door in the faces of my family and friends.

The greatest law is love and love knows no boundaries. It defies customs and culture and societal barriers. We must always be ready to be called into those special moments God uses. We must constantly look for

---

20. Again, Leviticus 15:31.

21. Luke 7:48

22. Story found in John 8:1–12.

23. Leviticus 20:10 states "If a man commits adultery with another man's wife—with the wife of his neighbor—both the adulterer and the adulteress are to be put to death."

ways we conform and make corrections to ensure our paths do not involve conformity.

Most importantly, we must be able to face the notion that everything we think we are doing right, may actually be wrong. We must have hearts and minds which understand the flaws of our own.

If we do not, we stand to miss everything the Pharisees missed when they stood before God and saw a lunatic. If we do not, we stand to miss Jesus in our own lives.

6

The Second Woe

"Woe to you, teachers of the law and Pharisees, you hypocrites! You travel over land and sea to win a single convert, and when you have succeeded, you make them twice as much a child of hell as you are."

MATTHEW 23:15

THE WORD FOR "CONVERT" used here is *prosēlytos,* or 'proselyte.' In the first century and before, the word *proselyte* described a gentile or pagan who had converted or was in the process of converting to Judaism.[1] Of this, there were two sub-categories of proselytes: 'Proselyte of the Gates' and 'Proselytes of Righteousness.'[2]

The first, Proselytes of the Gate, referred to converts who professed their belief in the one Jewish God but did not give themselves over to the Jewish religion. They chose to believe in only one god but not to participate in the many Jewish traditions and customs. The rituals and education required to become a full convert would have been deemed too much.

The second sub-category, Proselytes of Righteousness, referred to Gentiles who had been baptized and circumcised according to Jewish tradition and accepted the Jewish religion as their own. It is the latter category, those of righteousness, the word 'convert' in Matthew 23:15 is used in place of.

1. Matthew Poole, *A Commentary on the Holy Bible,* Matthew 23:15.
2. Matthew Poole, *A Commentary on the Holy Bible,* Matthew 23:15.

In today's churches, there is a large emphasis on discipleship. After all, the great commission from Matthew 28 is to "go and make disciples of every nation."

Discipleship is the act of teaching others how to follow and live like Christ. In layman's terms, it's teaching people how to teach people to follow Jesus. The term has gained popularity in the modern church in an effort to get back to the roots of Christianity. The biography *Daws*, by Betty Lee Skinner, showcases how the life and ministry of one of the great evangelists and founder of the Navigators, Dawson Trotman, was shaped by his emphasis on discipleship.[3] Trotman would refer to the notion of reproducing reproducers as the *"atomic bomb of evangelism."*[4] Using Second Timothy 2:2, the Navigator ministry became a worldwide movement of training up disciple makers.[5]

However, unknown to most people, the idea of making disciples is just as common today as it was during the time of Jesus.

In fact, John Gill's Exposition quotes Bereshit Rabba on the act of converting a proselyte: *". . . but [Jewish leaders] coveted to make them, because they either hereby strengthened their own party, or filled their purses with their substance, or got applause and credit among the common people, for the making of a proselyte was reckoned a very great action, and is ascribed to the patriarchs Abraham and Jacob, and made equal to creation."*[6]

While the entire quotation is significant, pay special attention to the last four words: *". . . made equal to creation."*

This act—of converting a former gentile into a believer in the one Jewish God—was regarded with the same reverence as creation. We hold discipleship in high repute today, but this is another level of veneration. While they would understand it was not quite equal to creation, (because this would've been considered blasphemy) this metaphor gives us insight into how important this process was in first century Judaism—it was high level stuff.

There are things in today's culture we can compare this to in order to more closely understand their rhetoric: winning the Super Bowl, winning an Oscar or Grammy, becoming a CEO, becoming Head Pastor, or winning

---

3. Skinner, Betty Lee. *Daws: The Story of Dawson Trotman*. Page 167.

4. *Daws: The Story of Dawson Trotman*. Page 270

5. 2 Timothy 2:2 says, "And the things you have heard me say in the presence of many witnesses entrust to reliable people who will also be qualified to teach others."

6. John Gill, Matthew 23 Commentary.

a gold medal at the Olympics. The prestige and pride associated with these accolades would be comparable to the ways Jews felt when they converted a Gentile. Glory is found in these honors the same way glory was found in creating a proselyte.

The process of making a proselyte would be comparable to the process involved in achieving the aforementioned accomplishments.

Winning the Super Bowl requires a life-long dedication to the sport of football. Those who acquire the title of Super Bowl Champion must eat, sleep, and live the sport of football. They must be consumed by it in order to play at such a high level of intensity and skill. They are potentially sacrificing a long and healthy life due to the well-known negative effects of playing the sport. Only the greatest groups of full-bodied athletes can withstand a full season of football to then make a playoff run to defeat another champion team from the opposing division. Only then, once a year in front of thousands of people and millions of viewers, is a single team crowned Super Bowl Champion. The life and career of a football player often revolves around this singular accomplishment.

Those nominated and selected for Oscars and Grammys spend their entire lives refining their crafts as artists. Many face rejection after rejection before acquiring their first role or record. Perfecting their craft and mastery of their art takes their journey to the grand stage. The road is long and tough and few end up at the top; but achieving this award is seen as the industry's top honor.

Becoming a CEO is the end-all-be-all of the business world. Many CEOs start at entry level positions where they work and work until promotions eventually land them in executive positions. Years of dedication and commitment in higher education and to a company are required to attain this title.

Head pastors are typically vetted and interviewed and vetted some more before finally becoming the head pastor of a church. The road to head pastor is not a lucrative career path and is attained through an intense and dedicated life of love and ministry. Many of those who attain this position live a life marked by servanthood and sacrifice.

Winning a gold medal at the Olympics is considered one of the greatest athletic feats in the modern world. The gold-medal-winning athlete is deemed the best athlete in their respective sport on Earth. This requires years of hard work and sacrifice at the highest level. Few attain gold medals, and those that do share in one of the rarest accomplishments in the history of the world.

As it was with the Pharisees, the process of making a proselyte was not an overnight accomplishment. The process likely began with a young Jewish boy who professed an innate interest in Jewish customs and the practice of law—either stemming from wishing to follow in his father's footsteps or from other outside desires. The boy's early years would have been dedicated to studying scripture and the laws while other children were playing. In similar fashion, one would give up a normal life and the pleasures that accompany it in order to become a Rabbi. Further commitment and studies and ambition may eventually lead one into the coveted role of Pharisee or a member of the Sanhedrin.

Once here, after already spending decades in devotion to the goal, the process of making a convert would begin. As Jesus says here in his second woe, the journey could often take them *"over land and sea,"* showing us just how hard these men worked to find and mold a proselyte.

Traveling over land and sea is easy today—we have cars, busses, boats, planes, and trains—and most people have access to multiple forms of transportation. Many of us travel longer distances in a single day than many people in the first century would travel in a year's time—and in many cases a lifetime.

During the first century, however, traveling was a completely different experience than any notions we attribute to it today.

Traveling over land was an expensive and slow undertaking. It also involved a great deal of discomfort and danger. George Mackie, in his book *Bible Manners and Customs*, states Jewish customs noted *"when a traveler sets out on his journey he must 'pay all debts, provide for dependents, give parting gifts, return all articles under trust, take money and good temper for the journey, then bid farewell to all, and be merciful to the animal he rides upon.'"*[7]

The Apostle Paul also gives us insight into what traveling in ancient Israel was like in Second Corinthians 11:26–27: *"I have been constantly on the move. I have been in danger from rivers, in danger from bandits, in danger from my fellow Jews, in danger from Gentiles; in danger in the city, in danger in the country, in danger at sea; and in danger from false believers. [27] I have labored and toiled and have often gone without sleep; I have known hunger and thirst and have often gone without food; I have been cold and naked."*

7. George M. Mackie, *Bible Manners and Customs*, page 146.

In John 11, we once again get an idea of how slow travel preparation was during Jesus' day. When Lazarus was sick, his sisters Mary and Martha sent word to Jesus: *"Lord, the one you love is sick."*[8]

During this time, Jesus was likely right across the Jordan in an area known as Perea. The distance between Jesus and Lazarus would have been close to 20 miles, which could have been covered in less than a day, albeit a long day.

Instead of leaving immediately, what does Jesus do? John 11:6 tells us Jesus stays there for two more days and then goes to see Lazarus.

This friend which Jesus loves is dying, and he has already healed the sick before . . .

Why doesn't Jesus go immediately? We know Jesus did this to show his power over death by raising Lazarus from the dead as he states in John 11:4.[9]

However, after becoming progressively familiar of Jewish customs, I also believe Jesus was delayed through his preparation for this short journey. As Mackie tells us, it would've been uncustomary for Jesus to hear about Lazarus' sickness and immediately leave. Jesus would have first needed to give parting gifts, pay any debts he had acquired during his time in Perea, and then bid farewell to those he was visiting.[10]

If Jesus' short 20-mile trip took two days of preparation, how much more time would the Pharisees' journeys over land and sea require them to spend in preparation?

In an era in which motorized and powered vehicles did not exist, the lone means of travel over land was either by foot or on a camel (or donkey or horse). Even if one possessed a wagon, this was ultimately pulled by one of these animals. Traveling by foot largely meant a maximum of 20 miles a day.[11] However, it was typically much less due to heat and the need to carry supplies.

Fred Wight, in his book *Manners and Customs of Bible Lands*, tells us *"a guide or someone who knows the way, and especially one who is acquainted with the locations of wells or springs of water or other watering places, is invaluable to the travelers."*[12] Wight is saying a guide would have been

---

8. John 11:3

9. Jesus reiterates this again in John 11:42.

10. George M. Mackie, *Bible Manners and Customs*, page 146.

11. Fred H. Wight, *Manners and Customs of Bible Lands*, page 371.

12. Fred H. Wight, page 369.

hired to make travel possible through difficult or unknown terrain. These guides further increased the investment required to make travel possible, as the cost had to include food and lodging for another individual.

Other than traveling by foot, traversing via camel would have meant quicker travel, with Arab camels being able to traverse nine to ten miles in an hour.[13] Traveling on a camel, however, would have been incredibly uncomfortable as a camels' movements are erratic. Wight informs us, "*the movements of this swift animal are hard on the rider, who usually prepares for the trip by belting himself tightly with two leathern bands, one just under the arms, and the other round the pit of the stomach.*"[14]

The rider would have tied himself to the camel and sat in a basket on the side of the beast. It was not uncommon for those traveling by camel to suffer broken bones and deep bruising during their trips.

Traveling by sea was also much different than what we may understand or expect. Daily scheduled routes between destinations did not exist in ancient times and, as such, people simply asked around until a sailor agreed to allow them to travel with them (for a price) in the general direction of where they were headed. Casson, in his book *Travel in the Ancient World*, writes "*Travelers did as they were to do until the packet ship made its debut in the 19th century: they went to the waterfront and asked around until they found a vessel scheduled to sail in a direction they could use.*"[15]

Casson further describes how Paul, during his travel from Caesarea to Rome, sought voyage on a ship whose final destination was the south coast of Asia Minor. Stopping at one of the many ports along the way, in this instance the port city of Myra, Paul swapped ships and hopped on a separate vessel traveling from Myra to Rome.[16] This type of leapfrogging would have been commonplace in order to reach one of the many hundreds of destinations dotting the Mediterranean. This leapfrogging also increased the costs of traveling by sea.

During the time of Jesus, the public had a great fear of the ocean and rightfully so. To extrapolate this fear of the ocean bestowed upon the population at the time, the Apostle Paul in Revelation 21:1 tells the reader "*the new Earth would have no sea.*"

---

13. Fred H. Wight, page 348.

14. Fred H. Wight, *Manners and Customs of Bible Lands*, page 349, Quoting J. G. Wood, *Bible Animals*, pp. 218–29.

15. Lionel Casson, *Travel in the Ancient World*, Page 153.

16. Lionel Casson, Page 153.

People would have heard this description and been greatly intrigued about the idea. While sailing was much less cumbersome and quicker than traveling by foot, many people still opted to travel by foot due to the inherent danger and unpredictability of storms and other seafaring hazards.

Mariners during the time of Jesus did not have compasses or precise maps of the seas to make long, straight voyages between destinations. As such, most ships would stay as close to land as possible to stay safe (weather is less volatile in shallow waters) and avoid losing direction. Distinctive landmarks and land formations were often used to guide the way.[17] The most common ships at the time were characteristically small, single-level vessels with no sleeping quarters; there was the floor of the boat and under that was water. Consequently, ships would stop at the end of each day at a port along the coast so travelers could find an inn or guesthouse.

From this brief description we can imagine how unpredictable and costly sea travel would be. The owner/captain of each ship would receive their share for passage on their vessel. Each day of travel would entail various costs for refuge at the end of the day. A towns' hospitality limit could be possibly overwhelmed, sending costs to an exorbitant level. It was simply unpredictable.

On top of these tremendous uncertainties is one that trumps them all: death at sea was common. Casson also writes about sea traveling at the time, *"writers fearfully bring up the mere finger's breadth of plank that separates a sailor from a watery death, and the farewell poems they address to friends departing for overseas sometimes read like elegies on their certain death."*[18] To risk traveling by sea would be to risk one's own life.

Point in case, to travel over land and sea would have been an expensive, dangerous, unpredictable, and exhausting undertaking. Our idea of traveling is in no way relatable to the reality of ancient times. The Pharisees would have been risking their lives and wealth to follow what God was calling them to do. Only men unreservedly dedicated were capable of such a daring enterprise.

What's more, whilst traveling, one would have to find a gentile who wasn't completely against religion and form a relationship with them. Following this would be countless studies and meetings to teach the gentile the laws and customs of Jewish life. There would be many rejections and failures as many gentiles struggled to adjust and adapt to the vast requirements

17. Lionel Casson, Page 150.
18. Lionel Casson, *Travel in the Ancient World*, Page 150.

of Jewish customs. Instead of continuing along the path to Judaism, potential converts would likely quit and return to their former life, leaving the Pharisee and their wasted time in the dust as a bandit leaves his wounded.

Nevertheless, after nothing short of a lifelong commitment to the One true God, one may finally be able to fully convince a Gentile to join the Jewish faith and participate in circumcision and baptism, along with the many other traditions. Years upon years, an entire lifetime, dedicated to bringing another person into the faith would have finally come to fruition. This accomplishment would have brought honor and pride, acknowledgement, and gratitude. Only the most dedicated and religious men could make a true "Proselyte of Righteousness."

This is why it was regarded as being equal to creation—because it took a gargantuan amount of work to make it happen. Only those solely dedicated to God could bring about a true convert.

Then, after you've risked your life and livelihood for the sake of God's work, some Nazarean carpenter named Jesus calls you a child of hell. Furthermore, he proceeds to call your protégé even more of one.

Say what.

Talk about infuriating the most powerful and influential men in Judaism—but Jesus was pointing out a huge flaw in the Jewish religious system and this same flaw is still applicable today.

The process of bringing an unbeliever into the faith is a crucial part of modern Christianity. In fact, some may argue this is the single most important part of our journey through life. The great commission given to the disciples by Jesus in Matthew 28 tells them to "*go and make disciples of all nations.*"[19] Today, one of the most important parts of my faith is sharing and showing Jesus to my friends who don't believe as well as any other unbelievers I encounter.

I am proud to say I have baptized a handful of people. In front of my megachurch I have dunked people who have looked up to me and have chosen to follow Jesus in part due to interactions I've shared with them. I would be lying to both you, the reader, and myself if I were to pretend I am not immensely proud of these moments (*especially when I've had people recognize me as someone who is often baptizing people*). In people's eyes, I must have it together and be solid in my walk with Christ in order to have such an impact on people.

---

19. Matthew 28:19

For some of those baptisms, I felt like I was following in obedience in my walk with Jesus. This appears common and is probably expected to be the case.

However, in other cases, the feeling of obedience has been far from the truth. Frankly, I have baptized people when I felt that I should not have allowed it to happen.

I am aware this is a very tricky topic to contend because who am I to allow and disallow people from professing faith in Christ? God has mercy on those he chooses to have mercy on, and he hardens those hearts he wishes to harden.[20] As such, I am hesitant to write about the following story. Nevertheless, I believe the purpose behind my telling is just.

I've baptized someone that I believed was being baptized for the wrong reason. As many men will understand, this male sought to be baptized in order to show a woman they were a true believer. This woman was spending a weekend in our city and the person being baptized had planned ahead of time to be baptized on that weekend. Deep down it didn't feel right, and when I asked them if they were only getting baptized to impress the girl, they replied "of course not." Against my convictions, I did not prod another inch and put my conscience to rest.

To make the matter worse, I similarly told a woman I was interested in to come to service that weekend to watch me baptize this person. Truthfully, I sought to impress her with my ability to bring people to Jesus as evidence that I had my act together.

I remember weighing the positives and negatives of speaking my mind, only to say nothing for the sake of impressing my potential love-interest. I cared more about furthering my own agenda than I cared about the baptisee's relationship and walk with Jesus.

As it appears, when Jesus calls the Pharisees and their proselytes 'children of hell,' he was also speaking to me. With this, I am not saying I created children of hell—so to speak—by allowing someone to be baptized. I did, however, refuse to show the boldness Jesus exhibited often in his daily life by speaking up in a situation that did not represent righteousness or integrity. I missed an opportunity to exemplify what it means to live your life marked by Jesus and to not put a potential romance before a relationship with him. I failed to show what it really means to accept Christ as Lord through baptism. I also failed to recognize the Spirit's conviction in this

---

20. Romans 9:18

situation, and, instead, chose to pursue my own agenda instead of what the Spirit was calling me to do.

Thus, I can understand how this woe applies to my life. And why Jesus rebuked the Pharisees in this manner. Furthermore, I can see why the Pharisees would have ignored Jesus instead of believing he might actually have something to teach them.

I am deeply saddened by this understanding as I share this story. How often I have thought that I was following God, when, in reality, I was further from God than I could have imagined. How often I have had this same realization as I study each rebuke Jesus gave to the Pharisees: I am no different than they.

How often have I been confident in my walk only to realize the confidence was for naught; that, in fact, it was this very same confidence that kept me from truly seeing Jesus.

The deeper I dive into this rebuke of the Pharisees, the deeper I see Jesus speaking to me. As the image painted in the introduction to this book continues to develop, I've noticed another figure standing across from Jesus next to the Pharisees in those temple courts 2,000 years ago.

It's me.

It's me two years ago.

It's me yesterday.

It's me today.

It's probably even me tomorrow.

I have not walked in repentance the way I should have. I have once again related more to the Pharisees than I have to Jesus. While this brings me sorrow, this has also constantly encouraged me to seek the power in this message. It has deepened my prayers that this book may reveal wisdom and Jesus to you, the reader. It has deepened my belief in why I am writing this.

I hope it has shown me the need to walk in constant repentance. As soon as I believe I've got it figured out, I must be willing to accept that I probably don't. I must be willing to accept that it is in my moments of greatest assurance where I may be wandering away from God.

Take a step, repent.

Take another step, repent.

Breathe.

Repent.

I want my walk of faith to be marked by this cycle.

Part II

If I can achieve this, hopefully, I will end up finding myself on the other side of the crowd in the temple courts 2,000 years ago, standing next to a band of dirty wanderers, rugged clothing and all, with my Savior and Lord in front of me, facing the same direction as me.

7

The Third Woe

"Woe to you, blind guides! You say, 'If anyone swears by the temple, it means nothing; but anyone who swears by the gold of the temple is bound by that oath.' 17You blind fools! Which is greater: the gold, or the temple that makes the gold sacred? 18You also say, 'If anyone swears by the altar, it means nothing; but anyone who swears by the gift on the altar is bound by that oath.' 19You blind men! Which is greater: the gift, or the altar that makes the gift sacred? 20Therefore, anyone who swears by the altar swears by it and by everything on it. 21And anyone who swears by the temple swears by it and by the one who dwells in it. 22And anyone who swears by heaven swears by God's throne and by the one who sits on it."

MATTHEW 23:16–22.

WHEN I ENCOUNTERED THIS woe for the first time, it appeared to me that Jesus was merely ranting as it doesn't seem to fit with the rest of the woes he throws at the Pharisees. I originally imagined Jesus to be filling space with words as he scrambled for the next bombshell rebuke.

As such, I skipped this woe before eventually making my way back to dissect it. In between months of writing, I came across the Talmud, the written Oral Law (followed by the Pharisees, *not by the Sadducees nor the Essenes*) as mentioned earlier. The Talmud is roughly 3,000+ pages (read that number again) of philosophical debating of the laws of Moses by many, many Rabbis. Thumbing through the pages reveals the remarkable intellectual prowess necessary for those who study it.

As you will soon discover, the Talmud seems to cover every imaginable scenario down to its many 'what-if' and 'but-this' branches. For Rabbis—as the Talmud makes clear—it wasn't as simple as declaring no work on the Sabbath.[1] The term 'work' needed to have a definitive meaning. Who exactly could work on this particular day needed to be defined.

What if a doctor needs to help someone on the Sabbath in an emergency situation? Is he allowed to save lives? If so, how does he make up for this work if it takes place on the Sabbath? What if a shepherd must tend to an animal giving birth on the Sabbath? Does he blatantly allow the animal and its offspring to perish, or can he work a little here and make up for it at another time? If an animal gets stuck in a fence on the Sabbath, do you help it escape immediately, or wait a day to help it?

Discovering and reading the Talmud exposed a side of the Pharisees of which I was unaware and led to drastic differences from the narrative of the Pharisees the gospels portrayed. As for the numerous times the scripture says Jesus was either debating or teaching in the temple,[2] one look at the Talmud and you'll come to truly understand what this means.

Take a look for yourself:

> *"The rabbis taught: If a sick person said, "Give two hundred zuz to A, three hundred to B, and four hundred to Q" it must not be understood that he who is mentioned first in this deed acquires title to that amount; and, therefore, if a creditor comes with a promissory note of the deceased, it may be collected from all of them. If, however, it reads, "Two hundred zuz to A, and after him three hundred to B, and after him four hundred to C," then the one who is mentioned first in the document acquires title to that amount; and the promissory note must be collected from the last. And if the money he receives does not suffice, it must be collected from the one mentioned before him; and if his does not suffice, it must be collected from the first.*
>
> *The rabbis taught: If a sick person said, "Give two hundred zuz to my first-born son so and so, who is worthy to have them," he may take them, and also the double share belonging to a firstborn. If, however, the sick person said, "Give him such an amount for his*

1. Leviticus 23:3 reads "'There are six days when you may work, but the seventh day is a day of sabbath rest, a day of sacred assembly. You are not to do any work; wherever you live, it is a sabbath to the LORD."
2. John 8:20. John 18:20. John 7:14. Matthew 21:23. Luke 2:46.

first-born privilege," the son has the preference to choose which is better for him—the amount bequeathed or the double share prescribed for him.

The same is the case if the sick person said, "Give two hundred zuz to my wife, who is worthy of them." She takes them and also what belongs to her according to her marriage contract. If, however, he said, "Give them to her for her marriage contract," she has the choice of taking them or that which belonged to her according to her marriage contract.

If a sick person said, "Give two hundred zuz to my creditor B, who is worthy of them," he may take them, and also collect what the deceased owes him. But if he said, "Give them to him for my debt," then he takes it for the debt.[3]

This is critically important! Pay attention to how the addition or subtraction of a single word can change the entirety of the scenario.

The sick person in this story is on his deathbed and these are his dying wishes. In the first case of distributing his wealth, by not using the word "then" or "after," the dying man is not attributing a hierarchy of who is entitled to their respective share.[4] This first case leaves each of the men equally vulnerable to ancient debt collectors (here-by referred to as a 'creditor with a promissory note'). If the debt was for 400 zuz, the creditor was free to collect the money from whoever he wishes: he could evenly distribute the debt between all three or he could empty Q's pockets to fully satisfy the debt or he could split the debt evenly between A and B, emptying A's pockets and leaving B with only 100 zuz. There was no definitive order of whom to collect from.

In the second scenario, by applying a hierarchy by simply using the words "and after," Person A is entitled to his/her share over B and Q; Person B is also entitled to their share before Q.[5] As such, Q is last in the pecking order and Person A is the safest. If a creditor comes to collect 500 zuz, Person Q would be the first to give up their share, followed by Person B fulfilling the debt with 100 of their zuz. Person A, due to the addition of two modest words, is entitled to their share as long as the promissory note was not greater than the combined shares of B and Q.

3. Rodkinson et al., *Bablyonian Talmud, Book 7*, Chapter VIII, page 307.

4. Rodkinson et al., *Bablyonian Talmud, Book 7*, Chapter VIII, page 307.

5. Rodkinson et al., *Bablyonian Talmud, Book 7*, Chapter VIII, page 307.

Part II

The teaching then switches to a different scenario under the same theme. To be noted, this passage informs us it was Jewish custom for firstborn sons to receive twice as much as other siblings when it comes to inheritance.

This new situation comprises of a sick man allotting money to others; the first specified amount goes to his firstborn with the expression of "*who is worthy to have them.*"[6] Following this choice of words, the firstborn is able to take the 200 zuz *as well as* receiving a double share of inheritance for his birthright. He is able to claim both amounts because his dying father did not distinctly specify what the amount was for. However, by changing the ending phrase to "*give him such an amount for his first-born privilege,*" the sick man is essentially assigning a limit to the amount the firstborn can receive as he is now forced to choose between one or the other instead of both. The scenario repeats using the man's wife instead of his son and is fundamentally the same situation. The lone difference is remiss: the amount owed due to the marriage contract. Firstborns were given a fixed percentage—double portions—while wives were allocated fixed amounts according to the Ketubah, or Jewish marriage contract.[7] The Ketubah protected the wife's compensatory rite in the case of death or divorce from her husband.[8]

As noted from Abraham's bid for Rebecca to marry Isaac,[9] Jewish men gave gifts of monetary substance to the families of their wives-to-be. This gift is known as the *morah*. In the Ketubah, the morah became legally defined as a debt instead of a one-time gift.[10] In the case of the husband's death or divorce, the Ketubah was a legal document noting the value of the morah to be paid back to the wife.

Taking the above and applying it to the Talmud passage, due to the husband's choice of words, his wife was either to receive both forms of compensation, or she could pick which was best for her.[11]

The third scenario described in the passage involves the direct dealings between a man and his creditor. If the sick man specified the amount

6. Rodkinson et al., *Bablyonian Talmud, Book 7,* Chapter VIII, page 307.

7. Maurice Lamm, "The Jewish Marriage Contract (Ketubah)."

8. Hayyim Schauss, "Ancient Jewish Marriage."

9. Genesis 24:53 says, "Then the servant brought out gold and silver jewelry and articles of clothing and gave them to Rebekah; he also gave costly gifts to her brother and to her mother."

10. Maurice Lamm, "The Jewish Marriage Contract (Ketubah)."

11. Rodkinson et al., *Bablyonian Talmud, Book 7,* Chapter VIII, page 307.

of money to be paid to his creditor but not the precise allocation for the payment, the creditor could take the gift and then collect further debt owed him. The sick and dying man, whilst on his deathbed, would have to conjure up precise declarations to ensure his wishes were carried out exactly as he desired and to avoid manipulation by those who heard him.

Side note, this explanation showcases the reason tax collectors were often despised in ancient Israel. A dying man is not typically focused on producing legally binding statements in his final moments. Applying the scenario in the above passage, a tax collector could be in a position to take advantage of a dying man and his family by manipulating the man's wording to suit his own agenda.

This imagery can be deduced to further understand the lowly position of tax collectors. A dying man's attempt to assign 100 zuz to his creditor could be twisted and construed to culminate with a 100 zuz gift plus another 100 zuz for the debt—leaving an already devastated family with further losses. The potential for exploitation was a temptation that many tax collectors simply could not resist.

As can be reasoned, implications from altering a few words in the comparatively modest passage above could considerably alter livelihoods for generations to come. As mentioned before, the Talmud contains thousands of such pages of teachings. Any further effort to dissect and explain the tome would turn this book into an expansive multi-volume encyclopedic work.

Words were everything to Pharisees, and the slightest change in wording could change everything. More so, a change in wording could spell the difference between a wealthy inheritance and bankruptcy, life and death, or even eternity in hell versus glory in Heaven.

Suddenly, the third woe starts to make more sense . . .

It appears Jesus may not have been as incensed about what object is sworn by, per say, as he is about their knit-pickiness in terms of sin and God. Jesus may have been angry that the Pharisees spent so much time debating what is and isn't allowed in their religion, instead of truly worshipping God. They spent more time arguing about how to worship God than they did praising him. They spent more time arguing over what is sin rather than repenting their own. They spent more time *telling* people to love others than they did actually loving others.

The Pharisees missed the point the whole time.

The law wasn't meant for us to attain, but rather to show us how incapable we are of being righteous on our own.[12]

Jesus, in his third woe, is calling them out for being petty.

Petty.

Sadly, this is a word synonymous with many in today's church. People argue over the race of leaders in the church. People argue over which songs should be sung. People argue over the age of leaders and gender of teachers.

Members distance themselves from family members with addiction. Churches outcast people out who get drunk.

Did you say you had sex out of marriage? You're gone.

It's the day and age we live in, and it's not much different than it was 2,000 years ago. The only difference is the change of subjects. Widows and orphans, while they still need care and attention, aren't the societal outcasts they once were. However, what about those struggling and failing with addiction? What about the transgender community? What about the entire LGBTQ community?

It wasn't the laws of God that transformed my life—rather it was the love of God through Christ. Instead of arguing over petty topics, there are entire communities of people who need to experience the love of Christ. There are millions of people out there who could use a helping hand and someone familiar with God's unconditional love; yet, instead, we find ourselves abuzz with menial disagreements. This woe can be used as a wakeup call to not be caught up in the small things, but rather to be reminded of what is important and what God has invited us into.

❧ ❧

The previous explanation of the third woe is rooted in a deep consideration of ancient Pharisaical values and beliefs; comparable to the use of parables in Jesus' teachings and allowing for various interpretations. It is a comprehensive study which paved the way for the above insight into Jesus' rebuke of the Pharisees. Not to change the narrative of Jesus' teachings, however, this woe is even more significant in its literal verbiage.

---

12. Romans 3:19–20 says "Now we know that whatever the law says, it says to those who are under the law, so that every mouth may be silenced and the whole world held accountable to God. 20 Therefore no one will be declared righteous in God's sight by the works of the law; rather, through the law we become conscious of our sin."

We've all been kids before, likely making up stories or telling fibs in order to manipulate. (If this did not happen to you, then maybe it's just the older brother in me.)

During the summers when my brother and I were roughly 10 to 12-years old, our parents created daily chore lists that we were required to accomplish before they returned from work. I noted that the lists were becoming increasingly longer under my name compared to my brother's.

Unsurprisingly, after weeks of this trend, I was fed up. I decided to wake up early before my brother and go down and *see the list*.

By "*see the list*," I mean "*rewrite the list*."

Thus, I distributed the tasks more to my own liking. My brother, while he is 20 months my junior, was aware enough to question why the lists were now in my handwriting.

I explained that mom simply called me and had me write down the list.

His response, to see if I was telling the truth, was: "Do you swear by . . . ?"

Now, as with most kids in my experience, the seriousness of the oath depended on what was sworn by. A "*I swear on my life*" meant there was an approximate 50 percent chance it was true. A "*I swear on our friendship*" increased the likelihood of truth to roughly 75 percent. An even higher probability would come with a "*I swear on my grandma's grave.*"

If an oath required 100 percent truth, the oath was sworn on the name of the Lord.

(You'll also find this in court when they place their hand on the Bible and "*swear to tell the whole truth and nothing but the truth so help them . . .*")

The Pharisees appear to have used a similar methodology when it came to taking oaths. As this woe reveals, the Pharisees were not much different than modern people. They knew to not swear by God's name,[13] so they used what they believed was the more valuable object when taking an oath. The Pharisees believed oaths sworn by the temple were only as solid as they were easy to carry out. The same applied to oaths sworn by the altar.

The Pharisees held the real weight of the oaths by the most valuable objects—the gold of the temple and the gifts on the altar. These oaths were unbreakable and binding; anyone who did not follow-through with them was guilty of a crime. John Gill's Exposition of the Bible says as much, "*This showed the covetous disposition of these men, who made nothing of oaths [which] were swore by the temple; but those that were made by the*

---

13. Exodus 20:7. Leviticus 19:12.

"Korban", or the gifts of it, were binding, because their interest was in it, it was for their gain."[14]

This, my friends, is a textbook example of idolatry.

Idolatry is simply defined by Google Dictionary as "the worship of idols."[15] Jennifer Slattery, multi-published author and founder of Wholly Loved Ministries, expands upon this definition in her article *10 Common Idols in Our Lives and How to Resist Them* when she writes *". . . idolatry extends beyond the worship of images and false gods. It is a matter of the heart, associated with pride, self-centeredness, greed, gluttony, and love for possessions."*[16]

Idolatry is discussed throughout the Bible—from the Israelites in Exodus through the Epistles of the New Testament. God makes his abhorrence of idolatry known in his first commandment given to the Israelites after their exodus from Egypt: *"You shall have no other gods before me. You shall not make for yourself a carved image, or any likeness of anything that is in heaven above, or that is in the earth beneath, or that is in the water under the earth."*[17]

One thing for certain, which is unfortunate for us, is this—regardless of how many warnings were given and how severe the discipline, the Israelites always fell back into some form of idolatry. Even after God struck down the nation of Egypt with 10 plagues and parted the Red Sea to free his people from over 400 years of slavery, his people quickly devolved into worshipping a golden calf they made out of their own gold.[18] Aaron himself, Moses' brother, played a crucial part in allowing this to happen.

The book of Judges tells story after story of Israel falling into patterns of idolatry, only to be disciplined so severely they end up begging God to save them. Once God in his mercy comes to save and rescue them, it is merely a matter of time before they fall back into some pattern of idolatry.

As Jesus shows us through his fourth woe, the Pharisees continued this practice of idolatry until the very time Jesus walked the earth. The

---

14. Gill, John. *John Gill's Exposition of the Bible.*

15. Lexico Dictionaries, s.v. "idolatry."

16. Jennifer Slattery, "10 Common Idols in Our Lives and How to Resist Them."

17. Exodus 20:3–4

18. Exodus 32:4 says, "[Aaron] took what they handed him and made it into an idol cast in the shape of a calf, fashioning it with a tool. Then they said, "These are your gods, Israel, who brought you up out of Egypt."

Pharisees held the gold of the temple and the gifts of the altar to be more important than the temple and altar itself—the very place God dwells.[19]

However, due to the Pharisee's vast knowledge of scripture and God's commands, they would have known his disdain for idols. Therefore, they would have done as they were to do and create laws against the practice of idolatry.

Unfortunately for us, this blind idolatry is not reserved to those in the past. Many would agree with the notion that idolatry has never been more prevalent than it is today. Humans have never had access to information and materials as they do today. Combining this with the relative lack of observable idolatry in the form of statues and altars has led to even more variant ways of idolatry.

I, myself, am no better than any man when it comes to idolatry. I have idolized more worldly objects and possessions than I care to admit.

When we define idolatry differently than the dictionary, we begin to see it is much more than "the worship of idols." Crossway, a non-profit founded in 1938 which publishes gospel and Christ-centered content for the purpose of leading people to Christ, adapts from Stephen Altrogge's book *The Greener Grass Conspiracy* when they write, "*We know we've become idolaters when a good thing has become a supreme thing. And the result of idol worship is always discontentment.*"[20] While identifying idolatry may be tricky in many instances, searching for areas where its byproduct has taken root—discontentment—makes it much easier to discern where idolatry is occurring.

As it is, my life has been a hodgepodge of discontentment. I spent years running from one thing to the next, headstrong in believing the next accomplishment would bring me the peace I was desperately searching for.

I believed I would find peace after finishing engineering school. After finishing engineering school and not finding the peace I sought, I believed purchasing a home would ease my soul. A week after becoming a home-owner, I decided it wasn't homeownership where peace was found, but in graduate school—so off I went to get my MBA.

Guess what I discovered?

Contentedness wasn't found in an MBA either.

19. In Exodus 25:8, the Lord says to Moses regarding the tabernacle, "*Then have [the Israelites] make a sanctuary for me, and I will dwell among them.*"

20. "You Might Be An Idolater If . . . ," Crossway, October 21, 2014, Adapted from Stephen Altrogge's *The Greener Grass Conspiracy.*

Next, I supposed I didn't have enough money in my bank accounts to warrant true peace, and I set out to build up a nest egg. To my dismay, the peace derived from hitting each milestone was quickly replaced by the desire for more.

I wasn't safe with $10,000—but it would be different with $20,000.

When I reached another milestone, the trophy of content was yet another milestone away.

Leading groups didn't deliver on the promise of peace.

Being in a relationship didn't deliver on the promise of peace.

Owning two houses didn't deliver on the promise either.

Neither did getting the job with the independence I had always desired.

Nor did the boat.

Or the car.

Or the vacation.

Or the bonus.

Or the clothes and shoes.

Or the social media likes and followers.

Or the assurance and affirmation from my peers.

Come to think of it, when my frantic search for a publisher for this book ended and I realized this book would come to fruition, my long-awaited peace never came. I justified to myself the peace would only come once the final submissions were completed.

The result of idolatry is always discontentment.

I used to work for a homebuilder where the sales staff was trained to find the pain in customers' lives in order to get them to build a new home.

Your backyard isn't big enough? New home.

Your bathroom doesn't have two sinks? New home.

Your dining room table feels cramped? New home.

Your kitchen appliances aren't as nice as your family members'? New home.

Your home isn't as nice as your friends'? New home.

These pains were curtailed to result in the purchase of a new $300,000, $400,000, or even $500,000 home.

Half a million dollars to solve discontentment?

I believe what many of us do is even worse. We spend things more important than money. We spend our time and effort and we alter our dreams and run down paths we should've never run down. We chase and we grind—because this world made us believe contentment is found somewhere other than within ourselves. Many of us spend our lives resembling a chicken with its head cut off, fanatically stirring from one thing to the next in search of peace.

Jim Carrey famously quoted *"I think everybody should get rich and famous and do everything they ever dreamed of so they can see that it's not the answer."*[21]

What a bold statement. *How can this be? Surely having everything we've ever dreamed of would bring us peace and contentment.*

My journey in writing this book has partly quelled my belief that peace and contentment are just around the next corner. By applying Santayana's saying,[22] I've supposed what I'm looking for is most likely not around the next bend. It's likely not going to be found in the next accomplishment—or in the next milestone passed.

It's likely not going to be found once this book is published.

It's likely not going to be found in the next job.

It's likely not going to be found in a relationship—or marriage.

It's likely not going to be found through traveling or the next financial milestone.

It's not going to be found in the next home.

It's not going to be found in the next anything.

If I don't have it now, I'm never going to have it. The stillness resulting from this realization has allowed me to see the blatant idolatry which has plagued me for so long.

I hope and pray the revelations explored in this woe develop to continually shed idolatry from my life.

There is only one place we should be looking for comfort. There is only one place we should be seeking refuge. There is only one place we should be searching for protection. There is only One.

The Pharisees did not understand this, and it cost them a relationship with the only One who could save them.

We can not allow things in creation to lesson our adoration of our Creator, the same way the Pharisees allowed the temple's treasury and the altar's gifts precedence over the One who dwelled there.

We can not afford to make the same mistake.

---

21. Jim Carrey, American actor/comedian when talking about what his journey to fame has taught him.

22. "Those who cannot remember the past are doomed to repeat it."—George Santayana

8

The Fourth Woe

"Woe to you, teachers of the law and Pharisees, you hypocrites! You give a tenth of your spices—mint, dill and cumin. But you have neglected the more important matters of the law—justice, mercy and faithfulness. You should have practiced the latter, without neglecting the former. 24You blind guides! You strain out a gnat but swallow a camel."

MATTHEW 23:23–24

FOR THE SAKE OF covering all this rebuke has to teach, we will explore it as two parts and then address it as a whole. The divide will be drawn between the verses, separating verse 23 from 24.

The year was 2015, the month May, and I was wrapping up the first of two rounds of senior year. I was fresh off turning 22 and my parents had warned me the time was soon coming where I would financially be on my own—no more assistance when it came to rent and other bills.

I had been baptized into Christianity and proclaimed my faith in Jesus as my Lord and Savior the prior month, April of 2015. I was moving out of a house I had lived in for the previous two years which was aptly called the "Toolshed."

This name was selected due to the inhabitants priding themselves on being what were referred to as 'tools.' Millennially speaking, we treated certain people with intentional disrespect when it came to relationships.

Moving away from this house as well as away from my intentional disrespect of women seemed to indicate that the tides of my life were changing for the better.

When it came down to it, though, I had roughly $50 to my name as I had recently spent all my savings funding my addiction to marijuana. The daily consumption of this drug held such a tight grip on my life, I couldn't escape it. Each night was spent spiraling downward from the high and swearing I would never smoke again, only for the proceeding day to remind me of the severity of the clench its consumption held over my life as I would yet again renege on my promises of quitting from just the night before. Those who have experienced this addiction will attest to the cycle one easily finds themselves trapped in.

Shockingly, it was at this time I decided I was going to prepare to buy a house.

A guest speaker at my church had recently given the congregation the following challenge: tithe for a year and see what happens. He then, comically, expressed his confidence in the lessons and blessings that come from tithing when he claimed his own church performed the same challenge and promised a full refund at the end of the year if someone came to regret their decision.

Even though it undeniably made little sense to begin tithing while trying to turn around the financial and spiritual tides I had been riding, I decided to take the preacher up on his offer and I began tithing in May of 2015.

In all honesty, what did I have to lose?

I was broke and addicted to smoking pot. The bottom seemed to be directly below my feet, financially speaking.

Long story short, I spent my summer working full time (and following school year working part time) and reading everything I could about real estate. I read about the different kinds of loans and the various pros and cons of each. I learned the difference between conventional loans and FHA loans, as well as 5/1 ARMs and all the other numerically-different-yet-same ARMs.

I learned how to get my credit established so I could qualify to buy a home. I read about what to look for in buying a home and what people regret most. I read about the best projects to increase a home's value and the most common mistakes first-time buyers made. Anything I could get my hands on, I vigorously consumed in order to prepare myself for home ownership when the time came.

Part II

I created spreadsheets showing how much I needed to save in order to afford a down payment. I studied budgeting and created a disciplined savings plan. I constantly looked at homes on varying platforms such as Zillow, Realtor, and Trulia.

Through this time period of working and studying, I consistently tithed exactly 10 percent of everything I made to the church. It mystified those who knew of my actions as to why I gave away 10 percent of my income when I needed to save as much as I could. To others, it didn't add up. To me, though, pride was found in my obedience.

Unfortunately, by the time the following spring (spring of 2016) rolled around, I had viewed so many prospective houses I decided to give up due to a toxic combination of overwhelming considerations and underwhelming prospects.

For example, the last house I viewed before giving up appeared to be a clear sign this moment in time was nay for my homeowner dream. This particular house was being rented and required a notice so the renters knew to be off the premises when we came to see the house. To our surprise and subsequent disbelief, the tenants forgot the date of our viewing and happened to be in the middle of throwing a party when we arrived. There were several people crushing beer cans on the porch as soon as we pulled up while simultaneously blaring music from frayed, rotting speakers lying next to them in heaps. Ignoring the warning signs, we still decided to give it a look over the loud music and handful of drunk strangers.

The proceeding five-minute walkthrough revealed others who were strung out on drugs and a woman lying face-down, spread-eagle in the first-floor bedroom, noticeably unconscious from some form of overconsumption. After immediately leaving the confines of the home, one of the men who had previously been chugging beers on the porch proceeded to beg me to buy the home and allow him to rent from me so he didn't have to leave.

I can't make this stuff up. I had seen enough in my opinion and was throwing in the towel. *It was time I accepted that now wasn't the time for me.*

In my mind, God couldn't have given me more obvious signs to move on.

However, within a week of giving up the home search and beginning the search for an apartment, a house came onto my radar which seemed too good to be true. I saw the home's online listing on a Friday, visited the house and submitted an offer on Saturday, and by Sunday the house was under contract—my contract. A month later, I became a homeowner at 23.

Through it all and still today, I believe tithing played a crucial role in becoming financially stable enough and being blessed with buying my first home. Along the way I was able to share my faith with others who couldn't understand why I would tithe while trying to buy a home. I often quoted Scripture in trying to get others to follow in my footsteps and tithe as well.

"Bring the whole tithe into the storehouse, that there may be food in my house. Test me in this," says the Lord Almighty, *"and see if I will not throw open the floodgates of heaven and pour out so much blessing that there will not be room enough to store it."*[1]

It's the only time in the bible the Lord tells us to test him, I declared.

Look at how he blessed me and rewarded my obedience. If you tithe, you will be blessed just as I have been.

My parents were initially confused by the way I tithed and they no longer saw the need to assist financially in the manner they had been up to that point.

If I could give it to a church, then I must not need their assistance.

What I viewed as obedience in the wake of clear opposing influence became a deep source of pride for me.

Look at me, I thought. *My parents aren't helping me as much because of my decision to tithe and stay in obedience to what the Lord asks of us. People have something to learn from me here.*

I gave a tenth of everything I received financially—work income, tax returns, work per diem, gifts, and I even went as far as to tithe any winnings from gambling. As soon as I received any sort of financial compensation, I made certain the first thing I did was to submit 10 percent of it to my church. I made sure I was tithing with cash at a time when many used checks and others had begun giving online. God was receiving my first fruits and I wanted others to make sure they saw the large wads of cash I placed in the offering basket.

I would go out of my way to tell people I tithed and why I tithed. I found ways to bring it up in non-related conversations. I began to believe those who didn't tithe weren't true believers, or they weren't taking their faith as seriously as I took mine. After all, if God is blatantly telling us to tithe and we choose not to, we clearly must not believe his Word.

1. Malachi 3:10

Part II

Over the relatively short time of a year, tithing had transformed from something I did not participate in to becoming one of my single greatest sources of pride.

It wasn't long until I found myself in the same trap as the Pharisees that Jesus addresses in this woe.

The sense of obedience I felt with my finances allowed me to neglect the less visible areas of obedience Jesus and the Christian faith were calling me into. The ability to show mercy, to act justly, and to walk in faithfulness—all those characteristics Jesus mentions in this woe; these were all things I lacked.

I would fudge my hours on my timesheet at work in order to bring home more to give to the church. I continuously lied in relationships to get what I wanted. I did not treat each person equally.

I call that acting unjustly.

I was giving up 10 percent of my earnings but not giving up those things Jesus was asking me to give up: alcohol and my still way-too-common drug use.

Sounds like being unfaithful to the more important matters to me.

Above all, mercy was lost on me. I became a black hole-of-sorts, devoid of the mercy God had so graciously given to me. I refused to show mercy to others. I judged those who didn't tithe. I distanced myself from those who didn't share in my faith in Jesus. I showed no acceptance for those vocalizing their struggle with sin. I condemned those whose ways were not aligning with mine when it came to faith.

Where was this mercy which was supposed to be a cornerstone of my faith?[2]

The Pharisees were just as diligent—even more so than I—in giving a tenth of their possessions as offerings to God. Jesus reveals they would divide up their possessions to the extent of even spices that they owned. This fits seamlessly with the concept of the Pharisees we've come to understand so far; their rigorous adherence to the Law of Moses and their fanatic zeal to continuously expand upon the Oral Law (Talmud) via discussion and brooding would doubtlessly have led them to divide up even the most nominal of possessions into tenths to give as offerings.

Having witnessed firsthand the pride in my own life from tithing, I can hardly begin to fathom the immensity of their pride derived from tithing.

2. James 2:13 says, "because judgment without mercy will be shown to anyone who has not been merciful. Mercy triumphs over judgment."

These men were spending time and effort to collect their spices in order to weigh their whole, divide into tenths, and offer it to God as a sacrifice . . . *as if God really needed their 100 grams of mint.*

It was their diligence and zeal in tithing which would have clearly separated them from other Jews and led them to believe they were closer to God than most. The inept pride from their diligence would've been nearly impossible to contain.

The Pharisees had clearly lost sight of the bigger picture, quite literally. Jesus uses the second verse in this woe to relay this concept to the Pharisees, but they are too caught up in their pride to understand the truth in what Jesus was saying.

Was Jesus tithing 10 percent of his spices to the offering? No.

Then how can someone who clearly isn't as devoted to God as us give us instructions on how to live?

"You blind guides. You strain out a gnat but swallow a camel."[3]

Relating back to a previous discussion about the importance of guides when it came to traveling—a blind guide would have been merely a simile as the adjective would never be used to describe the noun. Guides *had* to be able to see in order to do their job as landmarks were generally the most common form of direction.[4] As such, blind guides did not exist—if they did, they were worthless.

A blind guide would not have been able to get anyone to their destination. Even though the Pharisees would have been too proud to accept this, it is exactly what they were doing. Being the more progressive party at the time, people would have looked to them to lead them in the right direction towards God. They were essentially seen as the Jewish guides to God.

Yet Jesus tells them they are, in fact, blind guides—guides who have no idea which direction is the right one.

Doing what humans are intrinsically in haste to do, the Pharisees became so caught up in their own traditions they became blind to the more vital aspects of their God.

Jesus is using this woe to blast them with the notion they have lost all sense of direction in their faith. They are so focused on nominal duties they can't see the error in their ways. They are only symbolically pointing to the One True God, for they have clearly lost their way in terms of the more important aspects of the faith.

3. Matthew 23:24
4. Casson, Lionel. *Travel in the Ancient World.* Page 150.

Jesus continues to inform them they've done this by straining out gnats while swallowing a camel.

Once again, the Old Testament explains gnats and other flying insects were considered unclean under Jewish law.

> "All flying insects that walk on all fours are to be regarded as unclean by you. [21] There are, however, some flying insects that walk on all fours that you may eat: those that have jointed legs for hopping on the ground. [22] Of these you may eat any kind of locust, katydid, cricket or grasshopper. [23] But all other flying insects that have four legs you are to regard as unclean."[5]

Gnats can't be consumed, and this would be clearly known among the Pharisees.

Believe it or not, refrigeration and airtight food-storage containers did not yet exist in ancient Israel. Food was either heavily salted and dried, prepared and consumed quickly, or it was going to rot. Gnats would have been very common and surely thrived in and around kitchens and food prep spaces during this time.

Gnats waiting to feast on aging meat would have been attracted to the sugar in any nearby wines or teas. Due to their brains being the size of powdered sugar, gnats would literally kill themselves trying to get to sweet sources and would frequently find themselves drowned in pitchers or cups of sugary liquid. When the Pharisees and any other Jews would go to drink, they would first need to strain out any gnats.

When Jesus states the Pharisees strain out gnats, he was speaking quite literally. The Pharisees knew exactly what Jesus was saying here as he was only repeating an act common in their lives.

Yes, we in fact do strain out gnats to avoid being unclean before a clean and pure God, they probably thought as Jesus spoke the first part of this verse to them.

If they were to become unclean, they would need to cleanse in a mitzvah before being allowed back into the temple. As will be discussed in the next chapter, this cleansing was a very time-consuming ordeal. More time cleansing meant less time in the temple with God. Therefore, of course they were going to strain out gnats to avoid becoming unclean and thus being able to spend more time with God.

Then Jesus throws them a real curveball and tells them they swallow a camel.

5. Leviticus 11:20–23

Camels were yet another animal considered unclean under Leviticus law.[6] As such, the Pharisees would have never eaten any part of a camel nor drank its milk. Camels were only used to be ridden upon (or in baskets on the sides) or used as a pack-animal due to their ability to traverse long distances without needing to consume large quantities of food or water.

However, camels weigh hundreds of pounds and stand well over six feet tall; there's no way something quite so large could go unnoticed.

Or could it?

The Pharisees would have had no idea what Jesus was telling them through this hyperbole. Instead, they would likely have used this as another claim against Jesus' insanity instead of attempting to understand Jesus. This, however, isn't the first time Jesus used similar literary devices when conversing with the Pharisees.

Jesus says in Matthew 19:24, *"Again I tell you, it is easier for a camel to go through the eye of a needle than for someone who is rich to enter the kingdom of God."*

Once again, not possible in its literal sense.

In Matthew 7:4–5, Jesus, during his Sermon on the Mount, says *"How can you say to your brother, 'Let me take the speck out of your eye,' when all the time there is a plank in your own eye? ⁵You hypocrite, first take the plank out of your own eye, and then you will see clearly to remove the speck from your brother's eye."*

Yet once more, not plausible.

Why is Jesus saying these things to them? He knows they're not going to hear him out or think for a second that what he's saying may be valid.

From John 11:48 we know the Pharisees are plotting to kill Jesus and their plan revolves around using his own words against him. Ultimately, their hope is to catch him in the act of blaspheming. However, in the meantime, Jesus' similes and other literary devices will be used to convince others he is insane. If they can do this, they may be able to buy some time and get rid of him themselves before the Romans come and handle the situation altogether—something certainly no one wants to happen.

Due to the Pharisees' preconceived notions of Jesus' insanity, they missed what Jesus was saying in these verses and they missed what Jesus was saying through the entirety of this woe. The Pharisees were too focused

---

6. Leviticus 11:4 reads "There are some that only chew the cud or only have a divided hoof, but you must not eat them. The camel, though it chews the cud, does not have a divided hoof; it is ceremonially unclean for you."

on straining out the gnats (dividing a tenth of their spices as offerings) and were instead swallowing a camel (not practicing justice, mercy, and faithfulness). Swallowing a gnat is literally harmless, whereas swallowing a camel is impossible—yet if it was feasible, swallowing a camel spelled certain death for any human.

What is Jesus saying here?

Jesus does not want us to miss this. Jesus does not want us focusing too much on the things we think are important, whereas in the realm of God they hold little to no significance. Jesus is giving us a chance to avoid the same mistakes these guys made. Jesus wants us to quit putting so much emphasis on things that aren't important and which cause us to miss the bigger picture.

What could this resemble today?

What good is it to check off the box that you finished your daily bible reading if you aren't sharing the joy of watching an unbeliever come to know and experience a personal relationship with Jesus?

What good is it to ensure you're giving 10 percent of your income if you aren't pouring your life into the lives of others?

What good is it to attend as many volunteer outings as you can cram into your schedule if you're not present at home with those closest to you?

What good is it to make sure others approve of your walk with Jesus if you aren't filled with the genuine hope and joy that come from a personal relationship with Jesus?

What good is it to work a job that's slowly killing your soul just to prepare for a fantasy future that may never happen?

Jesus is telling us right here. It's no good—it's no good at all.

It's no good to get caught up doing the things other people want you to believe is important when it's not what God desires for you. God is far too big for us to get lost in the little details and miss out on who God is. He is justice. He is merciful. He is faithful. He is truth.

If these aren't defining your life and defining your idea of God, just as they weren't defining the lives of the Pharisees, you've got it wrong.

We've got it wrong.

Just like the Pharisees, we've all got it wrong at some point or another, and we are likely still wrong in many of those ways today. However, we can't allow these words of Jesus to just bounce off of us like they have for so long—like they did to the Pharisees that day thousands of years ago.

We can't allow ourselves to have a viewpoint similar to the Pharisees when they heard Jesus speak these words. We mustn't be quick to label teachings that appear radical as crazy talk—as nothing worth a second thought.

Due to the way the Pharisees processed Jesus' teachings, they heard his words and thought those words didn't apply to them, and, because of this, they missed him. They missed out on some of the greatest life-changing teachings the world has ever known.

These teachings include the 4th woe, which is to not sweat the small stuff. It's to not allow ourselves to get so caught up in the mundane everyday that we end up forgetting the wonder and enormity of the God we follow.

Don't allow yourself to miss these things.

Don't allow yourself to view these brief excerpts from my life as too trivial and refrain from relating to the teachings in this book. It's not the specific subject you should be relating to but rather the changing of the guard in the life of a believer, so to speak.

Don't allow yourself to fall into the same trap Jesus reveals the Pharisees were stuck in. Focus on those things that God tells us through Jesus are the most important.

We are to be living just lives, merciful lives, faithful lives. These must be what define our lives; the rest should not be ignored but should not be the focal point.

How are we missing them in our everyday lives? In what ways have we become distracted by the trivial? What are we paying attention to and how do potential distractions minimize our kingdom work?

We must also ask, what happens when we miss the bigger picture?

James 1:14–15 states, "... *each person is tempted when they are dragged away by their own evil desire and enticed. Then, after desire has conceived, it gives birth to sin; and sin, when it is full-grown, gives birth to death.*"

We die.

Maybe not literally—though eventually we all suffer the same fate—but rather figuratively. We live lives marked by death rather than life. We live lives marked by depression and anxiety rather than joy and freedom. We live lives marked by pride and self-righteousness rather than humility and repentance. We live lives marked by our own works rather than lives marked by Jesus' doings. We live lives void of the grace bought at such a price.

What also happens?

We live the lives of the Pharisees—only thousands of years later.

If we don't recognize who we are more alike—the Pharisees as opposed to Jesus—we are doomed to be nothing more than blind guides to those around us. We are doomed to live lives void of justice, mercy, and faithfulness; just like those before us. We are doomed to miss the wonder and power of Jesus living in us and through us. We are doomed to miss the life God is truly calling us into.

By identifying with those who missed out on these teachings of Jesus, we may be able to strain the gnats without swallowing the camels. We may be able to focus on what really matters. We may be able to know Jesus and to live our lives marked by those things which marked Jesus' life.

This is what I desire my life to be marked by: by justice, by mercy, and by faithfulness. Through identifying with the Pharisees, it's my prayer I'll finally be able to begin to live this life.

Woe to You, Me.

9

The 5th and 6th Woe

"Woe to you, teachers of the law and Pharisees, you hypocrites! You clean the outside of the cup and dish, but inside they are full of greed and self-indulgence. 26Blind Pharisee! First clean the inside of the cup and dish, and then the outside also will be clean."

27"Woe to you, teachers of the law and Pharisees, you hypocrites! You are like whitewashed tombs, which look beautiful on the outside but on the inside are full of the bones of the dead and everything unclean. 28In the same way, on the outside you appear to people as righteous but on the inside you are full of hypocrisy and wickedness."

MATTHEW 23:24–28

THESE TWO WOES ARE combined and discussed due to the similar nature of what Jesus was teaching.

Mark chapter 7 gives us an inside look at what Jesus was talking about with these rebukes.

"The Pharisees and some of the teachers of the law who had come from Jerusalem gathered around Jesus 2and saw some of his disciples eating food with hands that were defiled, that is, unwashed. 3(The Pharisees and all the Jews do not eat unless they give their hands a ceremonial washing, holding to the tradition of the elders. 4When they come from the marketplace they do

not eat unless they wash. And they observe many other traditions, such as the washing of cups, pitchers and kettles.)"[1]

Before eating, Jewish custom requires Pharisees and Jews to wash their hands and arms in a ceremonial manner. This type of washing is known as *mikveh.*[2]

Mikveh, when used as a noun, represents the pool of water where cleansing takes place. Mikveh is also used as a verb to represent the cleansing that occurs in the pool. In essence, mikveh is the process of making something that was once unclean, clean; and, as such, it has many literary applications. This cleansing applies to food, body parts, and utensils.[3]

A mikvah, in its purest form, is a body of water of natural occurrence. However, as we've discussed with the Talmud's teachings and the Pharisee's practices, there are many rules and regulations as to what constitutes a proper mikvah.

The following is an excerpt from the Jewish Virtual Library on the validity of a mikvah:

> *"According to biblical law, any collection of water, drawn or otherwise, is suitable for a mikveh as long as it contains enough for a person to immerse himself (Yad, ibid. 4:1). The rabbis, however, enacted that only water which has not been drawn, i.e., has not been in a vessel or receptacle, may be used; and they further established that the minimum quantity for immersion is that which is contained in a square cubit to the height of three cubits. A mikveh containing less than this amount (which they estimated to be a volume of 40 se'ah, being between 250–51,000 liters according to various calculations) becomes invalid should three log of drawn water fall into it or be added. However, if the mikveh contains more than this amount it can never become invalid no matter how much drawn water is added. These laws are the basis for the various ways of constructing the mikveh (see below). To them a whole talmudic tractate, Mikva'ot, is devoted, and Maimonides assigns them a whole treatise of the same name. The laws can be conveniently divided into two parts, the construction of the mikveh itself, and the water which renders it valid or invalid.*
>
> *The mikveh is valid, however built, providing that it has not been prefabricated and brought and installed on the site, since in that case it constitutes a "vessel" which renders the water in it "drawn*

---

1. Mark 7:1–4
2. "Jewish Practices & Rituals," Mikveh, Jewish Virtual Library.
3. "Jewish Practices & Rituals," Mikveh, Jewish Virtual Library.

water" ("mayim she'uvim"; Mik. 4:1). It may be hewn out of the rock or built in or put on the ground, and any material is suitable. It must be watertight, since leakage invalidates it. It must contain a minimum of 40 se'ah of valid water, and, although it was originally laid down that its height must be 47 in. (120 cm.) to enable a person standing in it to be completely immersed (Sifra 6:3), even though he has to bend his knees (Sifra 6:3) it was later laid down that providing there is the necessary minimum quantity of water, immersion is valid while lying down."[4]

More information can be found about mikveh at Jewish Virtual Library, but the idea is that many rules and regulations had to be followed simply for a mikvah to classify as a proper one. These mikveh were used often because Jews would need to constantly cleanse themselves if they contacted anything considered impure.[5] They'd also have to cleanse any cups and bowls and plates used for eating. It was an incredibly methodical process that required diligence and commitment. It was not taken lightly as one had to be wholly dedicated to the process.

In Mark 7, Jesus and his disciples are sharing a meal with some Pharisees who had traveled from Jerusalem to meet Jesus. When the Pharisees saw the disciples not following their traditional Mikveh cleansing, they called Jesus out for allowing his disciples to eat with defiled hands.[6] Instead of spending time to cleanse in order to not be made impure before God, the disciples dug in. Under the Law of Moses, the disciples were defiling themselves due to this lack of cleansing; they were unclean and defiled before a clean and perfect God.

The Pharisees had a point—if they were following what the Torah teaches and spending time dedicated to the cleansing in order to be presented holy before a holy God—*why aren't Jesus' disciples? Why aren't they following the rules? What exempts them from practices we've all been taught to follow?*

---

4. "Jewish Practices & Rituals," Mikveh, Jewish Virtual Library.

5. Leviticus has many verses which read along the lines of "[*when someone comes into contact with something unclean], they must wash their clothes and bathe with water, and they will be unclean till evening.*"

6. Mark 7:5 says, "So the Pharisees and teachers of the law asked Jesus, "Why don't your disciples live according to the tradition of the elders instead of eating their food with defiled hands?"

In his response, Jesus tries to teach them that they had come to use this tradition for themselves instead of using it to honor God.[7]

Jesus says, "*Nothing outside a person can defile them by going into them. Rather, it is what comes out of a person that defiles them.*"[8]

This is Jesus' main point in his 5th woe issued to the Pharisees—the Pharisees appeared to be the holiest and most-godly men in Judaism, but their hearts were far from God.[9] The Pharisees dedicated much of their time to making sure they practiced and upheld every law they could. They made sure they performed the mikvah before every meal, on not only their bodies, but also on each utensil used for eating and preparing meals. They made sure to stay away from people considered unclean—lepers, prostitutes, the sick and poor—so they could be closer to God because they were "clean" and "pure." Even their food had to be kosher—that is, 'clean.'

The Pharisees made it clear through their traditions and practices that they were the cleanest and most pure men in Judaism, and so they believed they were the closest to God of all the people.

"*The Lord says: "These people come near to me with their mouth and honor me with their lips, but their hearts are far from me. Their worship of me is based on merely human rules they have been taught."*"[10]

Jesus uses in this woe yet another jab at the relative blindness of the Pharisees. The Pharisees have once again taken an act of reverence to God and turned it into a meaningless tradition; and Jesus has had enough of watching these men parade around completely blind to the fact they have never been further from God.

As Jesus points out, the Pharisees have become so obsessed with ensuring the exterior of the body was clean, they were wholly unaware of how far their hearts had drifted from God.

Sure, these men smelled nice and were legally considered 'clean' so they could enter the temple, but their hearts were full of greed and self-indulgence. As Jesus informs them, there is no amount of exterior bathing capable of cleansing a deceitful heart. Jesus scolds their arrogance in their belief that God cares more about the cleanliness of the exterior than he does about the cleanliness and purity of the heart and mind.

---

7. Jesus' entire response is recorded from Mark 7:6–15.

8. Mark 7:15

9. Mark 7:6 quoting Isaiah 29:13.

10. Isaiah 29:13

The Pharisees were popularly known as the cleanest men in Israel, however, somewhere there was a disconnect—this sense of cleanliness was a facade.

The Pharisees have missed the mark yet again and they are oblivious to the notion of it.

Jesus teaches them they can keep cleaning the body, but until they fix the inside, which is causing them to miss God, all of their cleaning is useless—a mere touch-up on a villainous façade. It's all a waste. All of it. Until they correct what has really been causing their errant ways, nothing will truly change for them.

The same applies to us.

Romans 11:16 says this, "... *if the root is holy, so are the branches.*"

I don't know about you, but I needed this today—I need this every day.

For too long, I have found myself caught up in making sure the exterior looks good. I go to the gym so that my physical appearance will look good. I show up at church functions so people will see me. I make sure I check off the box of volunteering in my community, and that I'm spending time in the word daily.

However clean these acts may make me appear to others, real cleanliness is rooted on the inside. It is a culmination of life's happenings, woven together, and the way each experience has been perceived by the individual.

As we discussed in chapter 3, we must go backwards in order to move forward. Jesus is inviting the Pharisees into this; though he knows they will not take it. More important in this moment is Jesus is also inviting you and me to once again focus on the root. He's once more inviting us to focus on what's on the inside and to clean it up. It's an invitation to deal with the junk we don't even know is affecting us and impacting how we handle life's situations today.

I have gone on retreats specifically for this purpose: to clean the inside so the outside may also be clean. One of these retreats, located just outside Denver, Colorado, was so impactful I've pinpointed it as a major turning point in my life.

What I've learned in regard to cleaning the inside is this—it's not a one time reckoning. It's an exciting and riveting experience to overcome those things which have long avoided our attention and have long averted healing. Unloading burdens which have weighed one down for years is a staple of walking with Jesus.[11]

---

11. Jesus, in Matthew 11:28–30, proclaims, "Come to me, all you who are weary and

Shrouded in this excitement, it becomes easy to forget there is more, much more healing to be done.

I recently had a conversation about Jesus with a woman whose newly built house I project managed. She is over 70 and has worked as a counselor for many years, serving in churches and the general public. She confided in me about a question she posed to her own counselor just days before: "*Do you ever fully work through the things that happened in childhood?*"

She has counseled and walked others through traumas and situations which break my heart. And yet, decades removed from her own adolescence, she is still processing the way events from her past affect her today.

The answer to her question was "No," and this leads me to speculate how often this occurs in my life.

This woe serves as another reminder of what to pay attention to when things go awry.

When we find it tough to treat people the way we know Jesus calls us to, something on the inside needs to be looked at. When we find ourselves in the mood of all moods, it's likely rooted within us, rather than the common delusion that someone else is at fault for our feelings.

Many people take the path of the Pharisees and look on the outside for temperament—*maybe a nap will fix the way I feel.*

Maybe a Netflix binge will reset my mind.

Maybe it's a self-care day, and a bubble bath with wine will do the trick.

Maybe I need to cut those people out of my life.

Maybe a vacation will change my mentality.

All these things may help, and I'm not here to say whether or not they are right or wrong. Rather, I do have a question to pose: How have those done for you so far?

I know how useless they've been for me.

Jesus invites us to take a step back and observe our reactions; to observe what we believe about the way we feel. And then he invites us to challenge our own perceptions. After all, he's the one who created us. He's the one who knows more about us than we ever will and if Jesus is telling us we must clean up the inside, then we must do it.

---

burdened, and I will give you rest. Take my yoke upon you and learn from me, for I am gentle and humble in heart, and you will find rest for your souls. For my yoke is easy and my burden is light."

I desire to live with the love in my heart which Jesus had in his. I desire to live with the peace which Jesus walked in each day. I would give it all to live with the serenity which defined Jesus' days on Earth.

However, these won't happen because I bathed when I was dirty. Nor will they be the case because I impressed others with my ability to show up at every church function. They won't happen because I followed all the rules. They won't happen because I memorized a thousand bible verses. They won't happen because I received a Master's Degree in Divinity; or a PhD in Theological Studies. They won't happen because I led dozens of groups. They won't happen because of the titles I've earned or the amount I've tithed.

We should know these won't work—the Pharisees already tried them all.

My life will be marked by love and joy only if my soul is clean. Jesus showed us this.

I hope I can learn to take His advice more than I have in the past. I hope I can continue to learn the significance of looking within when the exterior world seems tumultuous.

A further understanding of the significance of this introspection can be found in the explanation of Jesus' sixth rebuke of the Pharisees.

The 6th Woe.

It was common practice in the first century to cover old tombs with plaster to make them appear cleaner and newer—and cause them to be more noticeable too. This is what the term "whitewashing" in this verse is rendering.

The Torah references the importance of remaining clean many times. In many of the laws, a person who becomes unclean stays unclean until evening.[12] However, when it comes to contact with dead bodies and graves, the time one was considered unclean is increased to seven days.[13] Uncleanliness caused by grave contact was significantly more serious. Touching the

12. Leviticus 15:18. Leviticus 22:6. Numbers 19:8. Leviticus 11:31. As well as dozens of other verses.

13. Number 19:16 reads, "Anyone out in the open who touches someone who has been killed with a sword or someone who has died a natural death, or anyone who touches a human bone or a grave, will be unclean for seven days."

grave of a dead person was considered as unclean as touching the corpse itself and there were stringent rules to follow after such contact.

> "*Whoever touches the dead body of any person shall be unclean seven days. He shall cleanse himself with the water on the third day and on the seventh day, and so be clean. But if he does not cleanse himself on the third day and on the seventh day, he will not become clean. Whoever touches a dead person, the body of anyone who has died, and does not cleanse himself, defiles the tabernacle of the LORD, and that person shall be cut off from Israel; because the water for impurity was not thrown on him, he shall be unclean. His uncleanness is still on him.*" Numbers 19:11–13

Due to the seven-day unclean period, a person stumbling upon a grave on the way to Jerusalem for one of the annual festivals would likely miss the entire festival. To keep this from happening, the Sanhedrin "*ruled that the graves and tombs should be given a fresh coat of whitewash in the days leading up to the pilgrimage festivals, replacing the previous coating that had been washed away by rain (Shekalim 1:1).*"[14]

In Luke 11:44, Jesus' rebuke in the sixth woe is recorded in this manner: "*Woe to you, because you are like unmarked graves, which people walk over without knowing it.*"

What Jesus is saying here is wild!

Jesus is comparing the Pharisees to the tomb of a dead person—in other words, they are causing people to become more unclean than any other unclean thing, and they don't even know it.

Inside a whitewashed tomb was a decaying human body, most likely half decomposed and giving off an unimaginable odor.

When Lazarus was in the tomb a mere four days in John 11, his sister, Martha, reprimanded Jesus for wanting to roll the stone back.

"*But, Lord,*" said Martha, the sister of the dead man, "*by this time there is a bad odor, for he has been there four days.*"[15]

This was after only four days. Try to fathom how much worse the stench might have been where the body had been decaying long enough for the tomb itself to require cleaning. When thinking about the most unclean places on the planet, the tomb of a dead person which has been there long enough to need the exterior of their tomb cleaned is at the top of the list.

---

14. Darren Huckey, "Whitewashed Tombs," *Emet Hatorah* (blog).

15. John 11:39

Regardless of how outwardly clean and righteous the Pharisees appeared, something else was going on inside them. Religious leader or not, Jesus' sixth woe to the Pharisees applies to nearly all humans.

We are quick to show off an accomplishment or to make sure the camera captures our best side. We make known the good parts of our lives, while keeping the dark parts as concealed as possible.

As Christians, we are even more prone to making it appear as if we have everything together. In our minds, we have God with us and he tells us to not be afraid, not to worry, and to be kind to others; believing in him means we must obey his orders.[16] We are to hate sin and restrain ourselves—just as Jesus did. However, our efforts to be a good witness to others creates many opportunities to whitewash our own tombs.

I have a deeply rooted love for the country and people of the Philippines. I spent almost three months living in the southern part of the Philippines during the summer of 2016. I volunteered in a village of displaced and disabled families, primarily taking care of the many children of the village. It was the best time of my life and I found more joy there than I had experienced at any time in my life up until that point. Upon returning to the states, I vowed to visit the Philippines as often as I could for the remainder of my life.

The following year (summer of 2017), I had the opportunity to return to the Philippines for a few weeks after a study trip in Vietnam and Hong Kong for my MBA program. I had two friends who joined me, and we had the trip of a lifetime. We swam with whale sharks, went scuba diving on reefs, climbed waterfalls, jumped off cliffs, snorkeled with millions of sardines, drank banana smoothies in infinity pools, rode motos through the jungles, and stayed in wooden huts and beachside resorts.

We did it all.

We took pictures and videos of everything we did and shared it online via our Facebooks and Instagrams. It was the perfect trip.

Or so it appeared.

Upon returning to the states, one of my friends saw me for the first time and commented along the lines of this: "I'm so jealous of your trip! You looked so genuinely happy! I wish I was as happy as you!"

---

16. Matthew 6:26 says do not fear. Philippians 4:6–7 says do not be anxious. Isaiah 35:4 says to not fear. John 14:1 says to not let your hearts be troubled. Joshua 1:9 says the Lord *commands* us to not fear.

I remember how shaken I was by this remark. She had no idea—in fact, no one did.

I had orchestrated the perfect optical illusion.

What people saw through my social media was not my reality. *It was not even close.*

My Instagram posts showed me smiling and laughing. My captions proclaimed the immensity of the fun we were having. I boasted about how grand my adventure was. I implored people to follow in my footsteps and live their lives to the fullest. I made sure people saw how joyful I was.

However, it was merely a false portico, as I was faking it all.

My mental health during this trip was the worst it had ever been in my life. Years of addiction and sin combined with an undiagnosed anxiety disorder culminated on this trip.

As sad as it is to reminisce on this lowly period, I share this information as an example of how drastically different someone's life may be as opposed to how it appears. Hidden from those admiring my trip from afar, I spent roughly every waking moment during this trip wishing I was dead. The darkness and hopelessness I was experiencing could not be shaken, and the only relief I found was by doing, doing, and more doing. We were moving nonstop for weeks. I was the furthest thing from being genuinely happy, yet somehow I was able to portray something completely different to those on the outside—to those watching my experiences through social media.

I was oblivious to what I was doing until someone confronted and informed me they wanted to be as happy as me. It blindsided me as I wouldn't wish what I was going through on my worst enemy.

How could my outward appearance have been so far from what was really going on inside me?

It broke my heart. To realize how focused I had been on making people envious of my life, instead of being truthful about what I was walking through, shattered my self-image and the façade I had created.

Why did I care so much about what others thought?

If people wanted to be like me, the only place they were going to go was a black hole of anxiety. If people followed my example, the only place they were headed was depression.

I was the perfect example of a white-washed tomb with bones of the dead inside.

Anyone who headed towards me and where I was pointing was heading somewhere I would never desire to be.

This is what Jesus wanted to expose in his address to the Pharisees: this false facade of righteousness and integrity. As Jesus pointed out, the Pharisees preferred a place of honor at the table and loved to be called "Teacher" by others. In other words, they wanted people to know they were important and how dedicated they were to God.

"Everything they do is done for people to see: They make their phylacteries wide and the tassels on their garments long; ⁶they love the place of honor at banquets and the most important seats in the synagogues; ⁷they love to be greeted with respect in the marketplaces and to be called 'Rabbi' by others."[17]

As much as I'd like to believe the contrary, this defines many of my experiences. It's ingrained in the human psyche—affirmation and acknowledgement.

As I've watched the Lord use the writing of this book to teach me countless lessons, I'm forced to face another reckoning.

What do I hope to gain from writing this book?

To help people recognize the Pharisee in themselves to allow them to understand and know Jesus in a deeper and transformative way.

Great mission statement, but no.

What do I really hope to gain from this book?

To follow a passion of mine (writing) and potentially create another source of passive income so I can pursue my dream of opening an orphanage in the Philippines.

A little better, but still no. Now really . . . What is driving me to pursue the publication and distribution of this book?

People to understand and fully know my story and what I've been through and to finally notice me instead of being just some one-off introvert that no one pays much attention to.

There we go.

Much better.

Affirmation and attention.

Deep down, I must remember this is going to be a desire of mine no matter how badly I try to ignore it or pretend it isn't. It's part of being human.

This challenging and raw realization has largely shaped the pages and narrative of this book. Each and every chapter has been revised and, in

17. Matthew 23:5–7

many cases, rewritten completely. It's through this revelation that I have been able to see how my innate desire to be known shaped the initial chapters and I've been able to alter and edit the chapters to focus on Jesus' life and teachings rather than my own.

The book you have been reading up to this point and beyond has been directly shaped by my honest answer to the question: what do I hope to gain?

Without this realization, this book would've read like more of a memoir instead of what you find it to be.[18] This book would have taught you more about me instead of Jesus' life—and pointing you to myself would've been failing you, the reader, in terms of teaching you that which could change your life.

And so, with these two woes, Jesus invites us to leave our desire for perfect appearances. Jesus doesn't want us to merely pretend to be okay. Instead, he offers us something much greater—the ability to be okay. He offers us the ability to heal and work on those things deep within us which have long surfaced only briefly to rear an ugly head in an attempt to win our attention. He offers us the ability to throw out those things in our lives which have once been mountains into the seas for good. He invites us to confront those things which rest deep within us with the opportunity to transform that which defines us.

If we don't, we're liable to become nothing more than what the Pharisees were when they walked around 2,000 years ago—decently clean, but fake and phony actors.

This is not how I want to live my life, and it's probably not how you want to live yours. I want to live a real life when everyone around me is merely pretending. I want to experience life, and life to the full as Jesus tells us he offers. As simple as it sounds, it's not easy or else it wouldn't have been a problem then, nor would it be now, with the added complexity of social media and our age of connection.

In order to do this, you have to be different. You must keep history from repeating itself. By identifying with the Pharisees and how they

18. Notice I say, "more of a memoir." I understand using my life experiences is going to cause this to read similar to a memoir. However, I have strived to replace many stories about my life with stories about Jesus'. Walking the line of being relatable through personal experiences, while mainly pointing to Jesus' life and teachings, has been challenging and required constant editing. I believe we, as humans, desire the affirmation and attention that comes from sharing our lives and stories. Accepting this has been the only way I've been able to turn from it. Show me grace, please, as I am still a work in progress—much like yourself.

missed this, we just might stand a chance. By challenging what is on the inside instead of merely concealing that which appears outwardly, we may step into the full life we are offered through Jesus' death on the cross.

We all desire full lives. It's part of our human DNA. There are multiple times throughout the Gospels where Jesus discusses the notion of a full life—made possible through a clean heart, pure soul, and peaceful mind.

Sadly, it is too common to find people looking for a full life in the wrong places. They search for a full life in money. They search for a full life through the opposite sex, or same sex. They search through indulgences. Through addiction. Through striving. Through deceit.

Sadly, I am one of those people. I have searched for it in many places where Jesus says it cannot be found.

It is not there.

It is only where Jesus says it is. It's with him.

As we move onto Jesus' final woe, ask yourselves what areas you've seen those you love search for a full life.

Did they find it?

Ask yourself where you've searched for a full life.

Did you find it?

How can you accept these teachings from Jesus' fifth and sixth woes and clean the inside? How can doing so enable you to move into the full life Jesus offers and so fervently desires for his people?

Woe to You, Me.

10

The Seventh Woe

"Woe to you, teachers of the law and Pharisees, you hypocrites! You build tombs for the prophets and decorate the graves of the righteous. ³⁰*And you say, 'If we had lived in the days of our ancestors, we would not have taken part with them in shedding the blood of the prophets.'* ³¹*So you testify against yourselves that you are the descendants of those who murdered the prophets.* ³²*Go ahead, then, and complete what your ancestors started!"*

MATTHEW 23:29–32

HERE—WITH INEVITABILITY—WE MOVE ONTO the final woe.

When I first began this book, I did not believe I would have much to say about this woe. I floundered and wondered what I would conjure up in discussion of this woe. I knew I would be able to find information and stories for four or five of the woes, but this is one of the woes I thought would only play a supportive role.

How mistaken I was!

As the book has developed and my knowledge deepened, the opposite has been found to be true about Jesus' seventh woe. In fact, I believe Jesus planned this one as his last rebuke, the final blow after his barrage of distresses, the closing argument to Jesus' prosecution.

As it turns out, this woe tackles with decisiveness the question which originally led me down the path to writing this book: "*Would you recognize Jesus today?*"

As I mentioned in chapter 2, my original answer to this question was "*yes of course!*" My faith rests in Jesus and I've heard many stories about him, so naturally I believe I would recognize him today. Before writing this book, I believed I would've fallen into the same category as the 0.01 percent of people who recognized him originally.

If only I were that special.

While I believe I am a special and knowledgeable human, I'm not ignorant enough to believe there aren't many more who are more special and more knowledgeable than I. I'm also not arrogant enough to believe I'm in the top 0.01 percent of intellectuals and Christian believers. Which means, contrary to what I'd like to believe, I'm probably not in the top 0.01 percent of Christians in terms of faith and belief. Which further means I would fall into the category of "*Rest of Humanity*" who didn't originally recognize Jesus.

This lack of awareness is what Jesus is calling out the Pharisees for in his final woe to them. This lack of self-understanding and humility is essential to the root of Jesus' final rebuke to the group of men who were supposed to know him better than anyone else.

The Pharisees dedicated their life to studying the Torah and applying its teachings to their own lives. Part of these studies included the great prophets who came before them—who had lived devoted lives similar to the Pharisees'.

They knew and respected the men before them who were chosen by God, and they honored them as such. Jesus tells us they built great tombs to show how great they believed the prophets were.[1] They also decorated their graves to show their respect and adoration.[2]

They further professed with their lips that they would have known better had they lived during the time of the prophets.[3]

---

1. Matthew 23:29

2. I have visited the tomb of Malachi and Zachariah, located near the Garden of Gethsemane outside Jerusalem, and it is a mammoth cavern dug out of a hillside in which both smaller and larger graves were further excavated to allow for the burial of the prophets' disciples. These were not simple graves and they exuded the esteem held by these men and those who followed them.

3. Matthew 23:30

They claimed they wouldn't have fallen in line with the rest of humanity and taken part in persecuting the prophets. They claimed they were different from their ancestors.

However, Jesus tells them the opposite is true and he is quite blunt. He tells them they are the descendants of those who killed the prophets and, as such, they should finish what their ancestors started!

Jesus is being downright aggressive in this final woe, and rightfully so. Jesus is not only teaching the men listening to him, but he knows his words will be written down and generations upon generations will study these exact words. If he is to express the importance of this rebuke to centuries of readers, now is the best shot he has.

He doesn't hold back. Jesus tells them they are no different than those before them; that, in fact, they too would have killed the prophets of age were they alive during their time. He even goes a step further and challenges them to do the same thing and continue killing prophets (AKA himself).

This would have infuriated the Pharisees.

As noted in previous chapters, the Pharisees were trying to trick Jesus into blasphemy so they could arrest and kill him.[4] They were actively planning on how to get rid of Jesus. He was threatening the safety they had created, and he was challenging everything they had learned in their lifelong dedication to God. Therefore, he was a danger and had to go.

By telling the Pharisees to finish what their ancestors started, he was talking about himself, as he knew what they were actively planning.

While the Pharisees might have played dumb upon hearing this woe due to fear of the crowds, they would have interpreted what Jesus was saying loud and clear: *"Go ahead and kill me. I'm a prophet and you're no different than your ancestors. I know you are trying to kill me, just as others like you killed the prophets before me."*

Now, this woe was not only applicable 2,000 years ago. Ask any and all Christians you know if they would recognize Jesus if he walked the Earth today and I have a feeling I know the answer: *yes.*

Unsurprisingly at this point, we believe we are different than our ancestors—just as the Pharisees believed they were different from theirs.

I'm here to propose to you we aren't—in fact, I believe we may even be worse. The Pharisees were men dedicated to God on a level we are not familiar with in todays' society.

---

4. John 11:49

The closest semblance we have for comparison is our head pastors. They live lives dedicated to sharing the Gospel, but their practices are no match compared to the traditions of the Pharisees of Jesus' time. They are not known for dividing even the tiniest of possessions into tenths and tithing them to the church. They are not known for ceremonially cleaning themselves before each meal or every time they enter the church building. They are not known for their ability to recite the laws of Moses verbatim.

Looking at the differences between Pharisees and head pastors, it's clear to see there are hardly any similarities between them. If these men were more devoted and knowledgeable than those we associate with being the godliest among us today, who are we to think we would stand a chance to see Jesus when they didn't?

We must be honest with ourselves, just as I've had to be honest with myself.

Naturally, we aren't any different than those before us. It is only through the Spirit where we become differentiated than those in the world before us (our ancestors). As such, we must walk in the Spirit constantly to help us not be caught up in the world in which we live. We must walk in the Spirit and ask to see the true character of Jesus. Jesus will always be rejected by the world, because he is not of the world.[5] Therefore we must be careful to not fall into the same trap as those before us.

Except if it was that easy, everyone would be different, and this is evidently not the case.

The path taken by Jesus was the narrowest path ever taken. In fact, it was so narrow only one person could fit down it—and he did it. As followers of Jesus, we must constantly choose the narrow path.[6] The further we go, the less and less people we must expect to find next to us. Through each narrow door lies yet another broad door and another narrow door.

I do not know what this looks like for each reader and I'm not going to pretend I know what the narrow path looks like because it is different for everyone. While we are all one body, we are many different parts of one

5. John 17:16 says, "They are not of the world, even as I am not of it." John 8:23 also reads, "Then He told them, "You are from below; I am from above. You are of this world; I am not of this world."

6. Jesus, in Matthew 7:13–14, tells us, *"Enter through the narrow gate. For wide is the gate and broad is the road that leads to destruction, and many enter through it. But small is the gate and narrow the road that leads to life, and only a few find it."*

body.[7] As such, we all have different purposes. At the end of our paths is Jesus, however, the road each of us takes to get there is different.

Due to this differentiation, the narrow road may look like many different things.

It may be giving up social media while everyone else is using it. It may also look like using social media when other people are giving it up.

It may look like staying in on the weekends while everyone else is going out. It may also change to going out on the weekends while everyone else is staying in.

It may look like finding a new community when your current community does not follow Jesus. It may look like joining a community of unbelievers when your entire community consists of believers.

It may look like starting to spend your time in church instead of outside of it. It may also look like getting outside the church instead of spending all of your time inside it.

It may look like setting time aside from your typically busy schedule to spend alone in self-reflection and prayer. It may also look like setting time aside to meet with new and old friends instead of spending most of your time alone.

It may look like getting behind a book or two. It may also look like getting away from books for a while.

Whatever the narrow path looks like, make sure it is different than those around you. Sure, becoming a Christian and following Jesus' commands involves a narrow path in-and-of itself. However, once you step onto the narrower path and look around, you are surrounded by another billion fellow believers throughout the world.[8] You are surrounded by enough people to form the largest country in the world.[9] You are surrounded by enough people to allow fame and fortune to be found.

While it's doubtlessly a good thing to join the family of believers, I doubt a couple billion people would recognize Jesus if he came to Earth today as he did 2,000 years ago in physical form.

---

7. 1 Corinthians 12:12 says, "There is one body, but it has many parts. But all its many parts make up one body. It is the same with Christ."

8. According to data collected in 2015, *Pew Research Center* numbers Christians on Earth at 2.3 billion people. The second largest religious denomination is Muslim at 1.8 billion. "Christians Are the Largest Religious Group in 2015," Pew Research Center.

9. China is currently the most populous country with slightly less than 1.4 billion citizens.

Therefore, even though by joining the church you are joining those on the narrow path, you must narrow your path again. Your path must continue narrowing until the only person on the path in front of you is Jesus. I promise you—that path is a million paths ahead of where you are now.

Nonetheless, it is there.

Each day is another path.

Each moment is another path.

Each choice at humility, of obedience, of love—these are yet another path.

The point is to be different, very different.

Be bold enough to walk the path of righteousness when those around you can't see it. Be courageous enough to cling onto the narrow path regardless of the trials you face. Be wise enough to recognize you may not know all you think you know; wise enough to understand you aren't much different than those who came before you.

Pose this question to yourself: *What separates you from the Pharisees?*

Is it your wisdom?

Is it your righteousness?

Is it your understanding? Or your level of devotion?

If you believe it to be any of the above, I propose you have been mistaken until today. Today is another chance at a different path. Another opportunity to step closer to Jesus.

The narrow path is this: to hold that what separates us from the Pharisees is our humility. To hold that innately we are precisely what the term "Pharisee" has come to designate; we are hypocrites.

It's our awareness of our humanity which leads to true knowledge.

"Do not deceive yourselves. If any of you think you are wise by the standards of this age, you should become "fools" so that you may become wise."[10]

It is realizations like these which may allow us to keep history from repeating itself the way it did when the Pharisees heard this woe but could not accept it.

Be the type of person who is so disconnected from the world that you may actually recognize Jesus, because he is here today.

Seek Jesus, and you will surely find him.[11]

---

10. 1 Corinthians 3:18

11. Matthew 7:8 reads, "For everyone who asks receives; the one who seeks finds; and to the one who knocks, the door will be opened."

PART III

11

Jesus' Conclusion

"You snakes! You brood of vipers! How will you escape being con-demned to hell? ³⁴Therefore I am sending you prophets and sages and teachers. Some of them you will kill and crucify; others you will flog in your synagogues and pursue from town to town. ³⁵And so upon you will come all the righteous blood that has been shed on earth, from the blood of righteous Abel to the blood of Zechariah son of Berekiah, whom you murdered between the temple and the altar. ³⁶Truly I tell you, all this will come on this generation."

MATTHEW 23:33–36

IN JESUS' CONCLUSION OF his rebukes, he once again calls upon his final woe to the Pharisees by charging them with being no different than those who killed the prophets.

I hope this book up until now has given you a deeper understanding of and painted a more realistic picture of the Pharisees.

These aren't the men we originally believed them to be.

These aren't the men we grew up being taught about.

These aren't blood-hungry men looking for the next kill.

These aren't the greatest tricksters of the time; making everyone be-lieve they are religious when they only sought to ruin God's plan.

These aren't evil men looking to deceive others for their enjoyment.

In fact, as you've learned, these preconceptions are far from reality.

These men were intelligent, loyal, and obedient.

These men sacrificed everything for God.

These men devoted their entire lives to bringing people to the One True Jewish God.

These men had given up the pleasures of the world in order to be fully dedicated to the Hebrew God.

Jesus seems to reward their efforts by calling them snakes.

Snakes were regarded in ancient Israel as the animal equivalent of the devil. Genesis 3 tells how Satan took the form of a snake and convinced Eve and Adam to eat his fruit—the fall from God. Satan tempted Adam and Eve into sin by not following God's commands, and when Jesus calls the Pharisees snakes, he is accusing them of doing the same.

The Pharisees would have immediately known what Jesus was truly saying to them. They would have known that Jesus was comparing them to the devil.

Jesus then calls them a brood of vipers.

Renowned Pastor John Piper taught on the meaning of this when he said, "*In Genesis 3, Satan is pictured as a serpent or a viper, and God says to the serpent, "I will put enmity between . . . your seed and her seed" (Genesis 3:15). When anybody said you were the seed or the brood of a viper, it was the same as saying you were sons of the devil.*"[1] Bill O'Reilly also informs us the young offspring of vipers were believed by the ancient world to hatch inside the womb and proceed to eat and gnaw their way out of their mothers' skin, killing her in the process.[2]

The Pharisees would have heard Jesus loud and clear—this is much more than merely calling them mean names.

He follows up his most recent compliments by asking how they are going to escape being condemned to hell.

The Pharisees would have gawked at this comment.

The Pharisees had kept the Jews safe from the commonly ruthless Roman imperial rule. The Pharisees had brought people into the temple and into Judaism who would've never been there before—they were the Robin Hood of the common Jew.

---

1. John Piper, "John the Baptist and the Brood of Vipers," John's Message to the Brood of Vipers.

2. O'Reilly, Bill, and Martin Dugard. *Killing Jesus*. Page 233 notes.

The Pharisees had dedicated their entire lives to God. Everything they did was in one way or another revolving around God—whether they were bathing to be ceremonially clean or cleaning utensils in order to eat, debating over interpretations of the laws of Moses in the temple courts, measuring their spices to the tenth to offer as tithes, spending time teaching their followers to create more pious Jews, preparing for long travels to seek out the next proselyte, or preparing to honor God through a fervent Shabbat.[3]

Yet in this moment, after all they'd been through and sacrificed, this treacherous carpenter (from their perspective) was condemning them to hell.

Yeah right, the Pharisees must have thought to themselves.

It would have been as near to downright blasphemy as possible in the eyes of the Pharisees.

Lastly—for the cherry on top—Jesus tells them all the righteous blood from the first martyr, Abel, to the last, Zechariah, will come upon them.

Jesus was saying they are guilty for all the righteous people of God that died before them.

When Isaiah was sawn in half by Manasseh, the responsible party was the Pharisees. When Jeremiah was stoned at Tahpanhes, the responsible party was the Pharisees. When Ezekiel was martyred in the land of the Chaldeans, the responsible party was the Pharisees. When Micah was martyred by Jehoram, the responsible party was the Pharisees. When Amos was tortured by Amaziah and martyred by his son, the responsible party was the Pharisees. When Habakkuk was stoned in Jerusalem, the responsible party was the Pharisees. When Zechariah was martyred by Jehoash, the responsible party was the Pharisees (this is who Jesus actually calls by name in his conclusion).[4]

When John the Baptist was beheaded by Herod,[5] the responsible party was the Pharisees.

The sacrilege!
The mutiny!
The sedition!
The despoliation!
The irreverence!
Little did they know—the truth!

---

3. Hebrew for "*Sabbath*"
4. Earnest Alfred Thompson Wallis Budge, *The Book of the Bee*, Chapter XXXII.
5. Matthew 14:9

What Jesus was implying was not that the guilt rested specifically upon the Pharisees themselves, but rather upon those who were blind to what they were doing. When the Jews stoned Jeremiah in Egypt, they did not know Jeremiah was a man called by God. When the Jews stoned Habakkuk in Jerusalem, they did not know Habakkuk was prophesying for God. When Herod had John the Baptist beheaded, he did not know John was the greatest of humans in the eyes of God.[6]

It is this obliviousness to one's own actions to which Jesus is comparing the Pharisees.

Jesus is telling them they have no idea what they are doing—they have no real concept of who he is, nor who God is. The Pharisees believed they were saving the nation of Israel from Roman destruction. The Pharisees believed Jesus was a crazed fanatic and a threat to their safety. The Pharisees believed they were serving God by getting rid of Jesus.[7]

Jesus, in his conclusion, tells the Pharisees they are wrong before they make their next move. Their ancestors were wrong before and they are only going to repeat their mistakes. This is something we cannot allow to happen in our own lives.

How can we pivot from things we've done in the past that we realize may not align with Jesus' teachings? How can we work to keep our hearts open to all God wants to teach us? In what ways do we need to turn from the mistakes of our own ancestors?

If the Pharisees harbored any inkling of doubt about what to do with Jesus of Nazareth before his conclusion, Jesus was doing his best to solidify their decisiveness.

6. Matthew 11:11 says, "Truly I tell you, among those born of women there has not risen anyone greater than John the Baptist."

7. John 16:2 says to his disciples, ". . . the time is coming when anyone who kills you will think they are offering a service to God."

12

Staying New

"Then John's disciples came and asked him, "How is it that we and the Pharisees fast often, but your disciples do not fast?"

15 Jesus answered, "How can the guests of the bridegroom mourn while he is with them? The time will come when the bridegroom will be taken from them; then they will fast.

16 "No one sews a patch of unshrunk cloth on an old garment, for the patch will pull away from the garment, making the tear worse. 17 Neither do people pour new wine into old wineskins. If they do, the skins will burst; the wine will run out and the wineskins will be ruined. No, they pour new wine into new wineskins, and both are preserved."

Matthew 9:14–17

The Tyndale Life Application Study Bible provides the following analysis of this passage: *"Jesus used this description to explain that he had not come to patch up the old religious system of Judaism, with its rules and traditions. His purpose was to bring in something new . . . The gospel did not fit into the old rigid legalistic system of religion. It needed a fresh start. The message will always remain 'new' because it must be accepted and applied in every generation. When we follow Christ, we must be prepared for new ways to live, new ways to look at people, and new ways to serve."*[1]

You've probably heard the idea behind this description before, nevertheless, it's the second last sentence which strikes me the most. "*The message of Jesus will always remain new . . . in every generation.*"

Applying this today provides for the following: There will always be *new* people who are societal outcasts. There will always be *new* ways to serve people and *new* ways to reach people. There will always be *new* methods for discipleship and new revolutions.

No matter the generation and the environmental elements which comprise it, the message of Jesus will always be *new*.

One of my favorite verses comes from Romans 12:2. "*Do not be conformed to this world, but be transformed by the renewal of your mind, that by testing you may discern what is the will of God, what is good and acceptable and perfect.*"

We are not to conform to this world, and because the world is always changing, we must also be changing. The process of being transformed, or made new, is not a one-off process—similar to how we've discussed repenting isn't meant to happen only once. We should allow ourselves to constantly be transformed and we should walk in constant repentance—this is the key to remaining new and grasping the full life Jesus offers.

I have been a part of ministries where the act of washing feet is used to show servanthood. Other than this, I have never seen someone wash another's feet in any kind of setting. While this is a good representation of the servanthood of Jesus, it fails to accurately present the importance of Jesus' gesture.

Washing feet in biblical times would have been a daily occurrence as the sandals people wore led one's feet to constantly become dirty. For those households which had servants and/or slaves, feet washing would fall onto the shoulders of the marginalized. This cleaning was an act of disparagement because only those from the lowest social class would be expected to perform it.

In John 13, during the last meal Jesus will share with his disciples, Jesus removes his garments and begins to take on the role of a slave. The act was so dumbfounding for the disciples, one among them, Peter, has no idea how to respond. He can't comprehend what to do and his initial reaction is

1. *Life Application Study Bible*, Page 1550, 9:17 Footnote.

to refuse the washing. After Jesus insists,[2] Peter then asks Jesus to give him a bath.[3]

This always makes me smile—imagining his confusion and bewilderment at Jesus' actions to such an extent he asks Jesus to fully bathe him.

This is clearly a man so shocked by Jesus washing his feet, he is lost. He goes from refusing Jesus' gesture to asking for the full expression of this act. He simply doesn't know what to do with himself nor how to handle the situation. This is how out of this world Jesus washing their feet was—the leader was never the one to wash feet, nor likely had one ever done so.

It confused them.

It baffled them.

Sadly, I'm sure it also *offended* them.

Nevertheless, ministries today use this example to practice the same servanthood Jesus asks of his disciples.

"Now that I, your Lord and Teacher have washed your feet, you also should wash one another's feet. I have set you an example that you should do as I have done for you."[4]

Remembering back, the Tyndale Study Bible reminds us the message must be "new." Extrapolating on this idea of being new, over two millennia the ways in which we serve others must also be new. As such, I think the extraordinary significance of the gesture is lost today in that it's no longer new.

It reminds me of a car trip I took with a coworker once. Within the first 5 minutes, he informed me *"I don't like to talk about people like this, but . . ."* and proceeded to talk about people the entire two-hour trip going and another two hours on the way back. The disparity between words and actions was so shocking it stuck with me—he claimed he doesn't do something and then proceeded to do it so continuously and unabashedly it was clear it was something he always did.

He said he wouldn't do it, yet he did.

I believe we use the act of washing feet in a similar manner, except the reverse of that example. We wash the feet of others' and think our service is done, as if we really did them a service in the first place. However, since

2. John 13:8 says, ""No," said Peter, "you shall never wash my feet." Jesus answered, "Unless I wash you, you have no part with me.""

3. John 13:9 reads, ""Then, Lord," Simon Peter replied, "not just my feet but my hands and my head as well!"""

4. John 13:14–15

people rarely have truly dirty feet in today's world, the act of washing feet becomes fundamentally pointless, merely symbolic. After all, there's no need to scrub crusted dirt from sweaty toes and blistered heels. Rather, we are lightly rinsing feet which have probably already been washed that day and then placed in a clean sock and a protective shoe. Washing feet is not serving anyone anymore.

When we believe our service is done by washing others' feet, we resemble the second son in Jesus' Parable of the Two Sons. Jesus taught:

> *"What do you think? There was a man who had two sons. He went*
> *to the first and said, 'Son, go and work today in the vineyard.'*
> *'I will not,' he answered, but later he changed his mind and went.*
> *Then the father went to the other son and said the same thing.*
> *He answered, 'I will, sir,' but he did not go.*
> *Which of the two sons did what his father wanted?*
> *'The first,' they answered."* Matthew 21:28–31

If we wash someone's feet but do not pursue other genuine ways of practicing servanthood, we are like the second son who says he will work in the vineyard, but does not go. We say we will serve as Jesus, but we do not go.

We say we will do one thing, yet we do another.

I am as guilty as anyone in that I almost always choose to serve myself over others. I have so many things to do in my own life—how am I supposed to find time to really serve someone else while keeping my own life on track?

Balancing full-time work, a healthy lifestyle, a solid social life, hobbies, building for the future, catching up with old friends and staying close to family—and still serve someone else's agenda on top of this?

Impossible.

Yet John 15:13 informs us this: *"Greater love has no one than this: to lay down one's life for one's friends."*

Jesus loved us greater than any love we could ever give and he laid down his life for us. While very few of us have the opportunity to go out with such an extravagant act of love, we all have the opportunity to lay down our *life* for each other each day. To lay down our commitment to work. To lay down hanging out with friends. To lay down pursuing our own agenda. To lay down our hobbies and #FitLyfe and chores. To lay down writing . . .

❧ ❧

As I've discussed before, writing this book has taken me on a journey of my own. I've been faced with the teachings of this book not aligning with life in its present state and the end of the previous paragraph goes to show what this has looked like.

In the middle of discussing how important it is to lay down one's life for others, I was met with the reality of how focused I had been to continue pursuing this book and how I was neglecting many people in my life for the sake of this calling. Had this happened before I began writing, I doubt I would have caught wind of the Spirit in the moment.

Do not get me wrong. I'm confident the message of this book is blessed and that by being obedient to this calling I have been brought into a deeper relationship with Jesus.

However, I also have been guilty of becoming so focused and dedicated to this pursuit that I've missed out on many opportunities to lay down my own life, so to speak, for others. I was not spending near as much time with friends as I worked to write this book. I was not spending time with my family as I sought to write this book. I was not seeking intentional interactions in the day-to-day as I knew I would be busy writing this book later. When I had the opportunity to have conversations with others, my mind was distant and my words shallow. I didn't have time to share with others because of how much time I dedicated to this book.

Yet in the middle of writing said paragraph now five paragraphs previous, the Spirit made me look at what I had been doing. Out of obedience, I put writing on hold and did not type another word for months. It was clear the Spirit had more to teach me before continuing.

I only point this out because this is *exactly* what happened to the Pharisees during Jesus' age and what I've discussed in this book. I was doing what I was confident God had asked me to do, however I had also gotten caught up in it to the point that I almost missed the more important aspect of disciple-making and laying my life down for others.

The Pharisees were faced with similar convictions 2,000 years ago when Jesus stood before them and rebuked them. The Pharisees were faced with the same convictions when Jesus told them they had no idea what they were doing, just like those who martyred the prophets of old.

He rebuked them for shutting the door to the kingdom in peoples' faces and not entering themselves.[5]

As I've discussed, I too am guilty of this.

He rebuked them for traveling across land and sea to make a single proselyte, only to turn said proselyte into an even worse child of hell.[6]

As I've discussed, I too am guilty of this.

He rebuked them for honoring that which benefitted them instead of honoring those things God declares important.[7]

As I've discussed, I too am guilty of this.

He rebuked them for giving a tenth of their nominal possessions rather than focusing on the more important matters God asked of them—mercy, justice, and righteousness.[8]

As I've discussed, I too am guilty of this.

He rebuked them for their phony facades where they merely tried to appear holy rather than becoming holy. He rebuked them for being fake.[9]

As I've discussed, I too am guilty of this.

He rebuked them for believing they were any different than those before them—for not being willing to reflect on their inherent wayward humanity.[10]

As I've discussed, I too am guilty of this.

They didn't listen. They ignored Jesus. They didn't give any thought to his words. They didn't think for a second his irrational teachings held any truths.

Don't make the same mistakes they did. Don't make the same mistakes I have continued to find at work in my life.

Ask God for help to find those things in your life which are old and need to be made new. Ask God for the wisdom to search your own ways and discern those which do not match the ways of Jesus. Ask God to make in you yet another new creation.

Then, a week from now, ask Him to do it again.

Be made new again and again, for it was out of complacency and comfort which arose the stagnant spiritual existence of the Pharisees. It was out

5. 1st Woe, Matthew 23:13–14

6. 2nd Woe, Matthew 23:15

7. 3rd Woe, Matthew 23:16–22

8. 4th Woe, Matthew 23:23–24

9. 5th and 6th Woe, Matthew 23:25–28

10. 7th Woe, Matthew 23:29–32

of this that the Pharisees were able to listen to Jesus predict their current moves and warn them against their future moves, yet still ignore Jesus and suppose him to be a lunatic.

While this complacency may originally appear as ignorance to the reader, this book presents an opportunity for all of us to recognize how the Pharisees came to allow this to happen in their lives. It is downright absurd that the Pharisees did not recognize Jesus as he predicted the future and expressed exactly who he was! Yet we are presented the unique opportunity to disallow the same mistakes the Pharisees made from happening in our lives. This gift, while difficult to grasp and fully comprehend, has the ability to continually alter our lives and perspectives as we become aware of our humanity in its full expression.

My hope is this leads to true peace and joy in the Holy Spirit. My hope is this leads us to see and experience Jesus when we would have missed him otherwise. This, my friends, is the hopeful purpose behind this book.

"For the Kingdom of God is not a matter of eating and drinking, but of righteousness, peace and joy in the Holy Spirit."[11]

We will never match what Jesus did for us, but he graciously offers us the chance to turn from our own ways and seek to live life more like he did. He has graciously given me wisdom in many areas of my life and graciously enabled me to share them with you.

Be made new.

Lay down your *life* for others.

Be like the first son—who says he will not work, but does—rather than the second son who says he will work, but does not.

11. Romans 14:17

13

Our Daily Ultimatum

IT HAS BEEN MY hope and prayer throughout the writing of this book that you have been taken on a journey of your own as you read these pages. I hope you have been challenged with reckonings long avoided. I also hope you have learned a great deal and discovered some areas of your life which resemble the Pharisees' lives more than the life of Jesus.

Subsequently, I hope you've been encouraged to pursue a life that more closely resembles the way Jesus wants us to live. It is human nature to live lives resembling the Pharisees' and it is only through constant repentance and diligent humility we may be able to turn from this and live more like Jesus.

As I've mentioned before, this book has taken me on a journey of my own, spanning more than two years and entailing countless life lessons. That journey has led me backwards through many things in my life which I believed were dealt with, when, in reality, they were still open wounds. While it has been both difficult and challenging, I'm confident the fruit from this journey will be blessed for the remainder of my life. From this blessing comes a gratitude and appreciation for the ways God continues to work in my life and I'm continuously praying for God to show up in ways I could never expect so that he might mold my life to become more like Jesus'.

However, the season I've walked through as I've been wrapping up this book has been much different than I was expecting.

The struggles and temptations I face on a constant basis seem to continue piling up. I've been walking through some of the loneliest times I've ever experienced. My anxiety disorder has been camouflaged to my own eyes. I know it's there. However, I can't locate the source.

I have also felt like a hypocrite as I've continued to uncover the heart of Jesus, only to find I relate so much to the Pharisees. As such, I've felt inadequate to act as if I have anything valuable to write about. It is this doubt which I've continuously wrestled with throughout writing as I find myself asking *who do I think I am?*

Who am I to think I have something to teach others—take a look at your own life?

Furthermore, writing is tough. Author of over 14 books, Joseph Epstein summed it up perfectly in his article, *Think You Have a Book in You? Think Again*, when he writes *"to be in the middle of composing a book is almost always to feel oneself in a state of confusion, doubt and mental imprisonment, with an accompanying intense wish that one worked instead at bricklaying."*[1]

Culminating at one of my best friend's wedding, my struggles caught up to me and I had to leave because I could feel an overwhelming anxiety attack beginning to occur.

The event should have been a great celebration as one of my best friends was marrying another good friend and I was surrounded by my church family and community, yet I can hardly recall it. Anxiety appeared out of thin air, drove me into the dark recesses of myself, and I felt trapped in my own body. My mind was not functioning properly to build memories as it tried and failed to process how to control the spinning labyrinth of anxiety.

I had to leave the reception discreetly as I was too embarrassed to say goodbye.

So here I am—years from what were without a doubt the most hopeless moments of my life. I stand confident in the sovereignty of Jesus, knowing what he has brought me through and the significance of what he did on the cross. Even so, I still find myself feeling hopeless knowing good and well that I shouldn't feel that way.

But, it's a different type of hopeless than I felt before I gave my life to Jesus. I'm still hopeful God will bless me with my deepest desires. I'm still hopeful God will bless me with a wife and kids. I'm hopeful I'll one day not feel as lonely. I'm hopeful this constant and overwhelming anxiety will pass.

1. Joseph Epstein, "Think You Have a Book in You? Think Again," The New York Times.

However, even if God doesn't bless me with those things, I will still praise him. Even if I spend my life alone. Even if the anxiety never leaves. Even if things don't pan out the way I envisioned they would when I initially came to God for help.

I will always follow Jesus.

Which is where that feeling I can't describe comes from—knowing he has the authority and ability to bless me with the things I desire, but also understanding that's not what following him means.

It's this, my friends, which has been a tough pill to swallow. To be honest, I came to faith initially seeking a happy life and the things I thought God would give me if I obeyed him. Rather, as my knowledge of Jesus has grown, so has my understanding of what it means to follow him. We are told it's going to be difficult and we will struggle and labor in this life,[2] but we like to downplay the reality and significance of this.

(The Pharisees definitely did not understand the depth of what this means.)

In Chapter 10 we reviewed the final woe of seven, where Jesus accuses the Pharisees of being no different than their ancestors. If we do not apply the same mentality today, who are we to believe we will be any different from our own ancestors—those who killed Jesus? It has been an endless cycle which we must recognize in order to keep history from repeating itself.

Yes, we will struggle and be excluded from the world when we leave our life of sin behind us, but we will be accepted by the church. We will be accepted by those who have also left their lives of sin. However, (*and take this with a grain of salt*) what happens when the church becomes a smaller version of the world?

What happens when the church is large enough to find fame and fortune? What happens when one can pass off wealth and comfort as being blessed by God for following him—just as the Pharisees believed? What happens when we believe these blessings are earned because of what we've done and how we've lived?

The God we worship is one who blesses those who love him, so how can we tell the difference between God's blessings and earned blessings?

As we've learned, Jesus was mocked, beaten, and killed by the most respected and wise leaders of the church of the time. What if the same thing applies to us today as followers of Jesus?

---

2. John 16:33 says, "I have told you these things, so that in me you may have peace. In this world you will have trouble. But take heart! I have overcome the world."

What if in order to truly follow Jesus we must be different, and much more so, than other people in the church? What if we must be so different that members of the church are confused by our actions and feel exposed by us? Other adjectives used to describe how others might feel by our actions could be susceptible, threatened, endangered, and vulnerable.

This is what happened to Jesus and his followers.

I do not write this to accuse churches of being comprised of people who don't know Jesus. On the contrary, I know the same spirit that is in Jesus lives in me and in anyone who calls on his name.[3] It just so happens that when the facts are laid before us, the church at the time missed Jesus. (I understand that the church today is different from the 'church' in Jesus' day—this is only meant to pose an idea.)

As such, we must keep this notion in our mind—as soon as everyone around us appears to be comfortable and conforming to similar ideas and ways of walking with Jesus, we must move ahead or we are in danger of falling into the same trap as the church before us.

Would you be okay accepting a life as an outcast?

Of being mocked?

Of being rejected?

Not only by those in the world, but also by those in the church.

If this is the reality you were facing—and this should be the reality you are facing—would you be okay with it? Are you okay with it?

The Father asked Jesus to do just this—to experience rejection, humiliation, and hatred by both the world and the church—and he stayed obedient to the point of death.

He stayed obedient because he knew we couldn't.

With his life, Jesus paid for our eternity. He paid the price so even if we live a thoroughly difficult life this side of heaven, our eternity is secured with him in glory.

Knowing this, I must be willing to live like Jesus did. I don't have to do this, but I am. And so I think the feeling I've experienced from the realization is similar to what Jesus experienced in the shortest verse in the bible.

"He wept."[4]

---

3. Romans 10:12–13 says, "For there is no difference between Jew and Gentile—the same Lord is Lord of all and richly blesses all who call on him, 13 for, "Everyone who calls on the name of the Lord will be saved."

4. John 11:35.

He knew he was about to raise Lazarus from the dead, but he wept anyway.

I know what eternity holds for me, but this life is hard.

What about Jesus in the Garden of Gethsemane? His sweat was like blood he was so stressed.[5] Even though he was God and knew he would rise from the grave to conquer death, he was overcome with anxiety. He was about to redeem humanity for eternity and his emotions weren't ones of excitement.

Listen to the reality of this statement: Jesus—God—was within days of conquering the sin and death which had plagued mankind since the fall—the greatest act of love in the history of earth—to prove himself as the Almighty to be glorified forever, yet he was so anxious his body underwent hematidrosis (sweating blood).[6]

This is what I feel like—knowing the promise of eternity but feeling overwhelmed by the potential hardship I'll face in this life.

It's my hope and prayer that my experience on earth won't be void of the blessings I desire. At the same time, if my hope rests in the fulfillment of my desires, my hope isn't based on Jesus. Hope that isn't based on Jesus is not hope at all. I don't seek a faith in Jesus that rests upon expecting him to bring my desires to fruition. My faith is based upon Jesus rising from the grave to give humanity the free opportunity to be redeemed back to God by only believing in him.

This is the most gracious thing I could ever ask for.

As for this, I desire my joy to be found on the other side of this life. Having been given the most gracious gift imaginable, any blessings gifted in this life are a testament to his abundant grace and can't be expected.

What it boils down to is this—what do you do when God's plan for your life contradicts the desires you came to God seeking? I understand it's a selfish and challenging question, but we must be honest with the answer.

What if your dream is to be pastor of a megachurch, but God's plan for you is to succumb to cancer and be a witness to your nurses as they care for you?

---

5. Luke 22:44 says, "And being in anguish, he prayed more earnestly, and his sweat was like drops of blood falling to the ground."

6. While Jesus sweating blood is one of the most notorious cases, Jacalyn Duffin writes, "*As early as the third century B.C., two treatises by Aristotle contained passages about sweat that either looked like, or really was, blood.*" Jacalyn Duffin, "Sweating Blood: History and Review," *Canadian Medical Association Journal* 189, no. 42.

What if you desired children and a spouse and to raise them in the faith, but God called your family to heaven too soon, leaving you a widow who seeks other widows as you all walk together through lifes' toughest moments?

What if you wish to be a missionary and open an orphanage in a third world country, but God's desire is for you to work a nine-to-five job under a difficult boss for 30 years and continually witness to him/her?

What if you desire to live in the upper end of town where your friends and family live, but God's desire is for you to live in an impoverished community to share the good news of Christ with those less fortunate?

What if your dreams include a long and healthy life, but a tragic accident leaves you handicapped? Is it possible to be a beacon of hope when your health is snatched away for good?

This is real. This is very real.

These are questions you must ask yourself. What happens when you face the reality of choosing God's plan or your own?

It's easy to say it, however, it's an entirely different story to put faith into practice.

It's my hope and prayer that when I face those moments, I remember what Jesus did on the cross and how he sealed my eternity. So, if I must give up this life, I hope I have the strength and courage to submit to God's plans.

It's my hope and prayer that when you find yourself in such moments, you will find the same strength Jesus had to stand up in the Garden of Gethsemane, wipe his bloody sweat from his face, and walk towards Calvary.

The glory we are to experience with Christ in heaven is greater than anything we can imagine or fathom—trumping all sufferings and trials we will face on this side of heaven. It is this hope which is greater than the sum of all our pains and anguishes in the world.

"I consider that our present sufferings are not worth comparing to the glory that will be revealed in us."[7]

---

7. Romans 8:18

14

The Four Soils and You

ALL DEPRESSING THOUGHTS ASIDE, I'm not saying a life of difficulty will be the case for all, or even most of us. Nevertheless, the significance of your reaction to the notion of contradictory plans can't be lost or ignored.

It was the ulterior reaction from the religious leaders of Jesus' time that influenced the way we view the Pharisees today. Their answer to the question posed before—*what do you do when God's plans for your life directly contradict what you've long desired*—changed the meaning of their title from respected church leader, to hypocrite. The Pharisees went from the closest to God, to plotting the murder of Jesus.

How is such a drastic divergence possible?

How did such extremely intelligent humans allow this to happen in their lives?

Part of the answer is this—God's plans for the Pharisees didn't align with what they expected.

It did not involve comfort.

It did not involve pleasure.

It involved neither wealth nor riches.

It was not rooted in safety.

It did not involve popularity or notoriety, fame or glory.

Instead, God's plan involved servanthood and rejection.

It required boundless humility.

Instead of riches and glory, it involved poverty, danger, and persecution.

The Pharisees weren't ready for that. They didn't submit to it and, instead, rejected it. Because of this, they missed out on God.

Throughout the studies and revelations which have culminated in this book, I've come to understand how much I relate to the Pharisees instead of relating to Jesus. I've discovered it's my innate nature to react the same way the Pharisees would and did.

Now, being able to comprehend this, I'm ready for this to change and I desire wisdom and boldness to move from "hoping" to action. I'm ready to apply the teachings from this book to every aspect of my life. I'm ready to understand that when I think I'm right, I may very well be wrong. I'm ready to see a deeper, transformed life from constantly walking in repentance. I'm ready to lay down my life in order to truly serve others. I'm ready to receive Jesus' rebukes to the Pharisees as they apply to my own life.

Notably, I also am ready to watch how I fail at these endeavors because of my innate nature, (*because I know it's going to happen*) and to once again learn and redirect my life closer to Jesus.

I can only begin to fathom how different the Pharisees' lives would have been had they accepted Jesus as he was, and it excites me to have the ability to step into it. If they had, the term 'pharisee' may mean something completely different today.

Hypothetically, it may have been an adjective to describe 'one who serves,' or 'one who lives a life of honor.' Instead, we have its present meaning of hypocrite. One day, many centuries from now, I hope those things I've been a part of do not have their meanings devolve into such antagonistic terms.

ⷱ ⷱ

I believe the best way to wrap up this book is to explore one of the most popularly used and spoken parables of Jesus—The Parable of the Four Soils.[1] Of equal significance is Mark found Jesus' explanation of this parable so important that he also included it in his gospel writings.

> "*Again Jesus began to teach by the lake. The crowd that gathered around him was so large that he got into a boat and sat in it out on the lake, while all the people were along the shore at the water's edge.*
> *2He taught them many things by parables, and in his teaching said:*
> *3"Listen! A farmer went out to sow his seed. 4As he was scattering the seed, some fell along the path, and the birds came and ate it up.*

---

1. Mark 4:1–25

5Some fell on rocky places, where it did not have much soil. It sprang up quickly, because the soil was shallow. 6But when the sun came up, the plants were scorched, and they withered because they had no root. 7Other seed fell among thorns, which grew up and choked the plants, so that they did not bear grain. 8Still other seed fell on good soil. It came up, grew and produced a crop, some multiplying thirty, some sixty, some a hundred times."

9Then Jesus said, "Whoever has ears to hear, let them hear."

10When he was alone, the Twelve and the others around him asked him about the parables. 11He told them, "The secret of the kingdom of God has been given to you. But to those on the outside everything is said in parables 12so that,

"'they may be ever seeing but never perceiving,
and ever hearing but never understanding;
otherwise they might turn and be forgiven!'"2

13Then Jesus said to them, "Don't you understand this parable? How then will you understand any parable? 14The farmer sows the word. 15Some people are like seed along the path, where the word is sown. As soon as they hear it, Satan comes and takes away the word that was sown in them. 16Others, like seed sown on rocky places, hear the word and at once receive it with joy. 17But since they have no root, they last only a short time. When trouble or persecution comes because of the word, they quickly fall away. 18Still others, like seed sown among thorns, hear the word; 19but the worries of this life, the deceitfulness of wealth and the desires for other things come in and choke the word, making it unfruitful. 20Others, like seed sown on good soil, hear the word, accept it, and produce a crop—some thirty, some sixty, some a hundred times what was sown."

Growing up, I heard this parable taught in church and religion class and it was in my children's picture Bible as well—so this is a passage I have been taught and heard throughout my life. Throughout my life, had I been asked which soil am I, I would've proudly declared that I am the good soil.

Through years of bullying my little brother, the good soil.

Through years of watching pornography, the good soil.

Through years of constant lying and deceit, the good soil.

Through years of alcohol and drug abuse, the good soil.

Through years of infidelity and sexual immorality, the good soil.

Through years of battling and losing to depression, the good soil.

---

2. This quotes Isaiah 6:9: *"He said, "Go and tell this people: "'Be ever hearing, but never understanding; be ever seeing, but never perceiving.'"*

Through years of unhealthy relationships, the good soil.

And even once I found Christ . . .

The years of pride rooted in all I had sacrificed, good soil.

The years of sobriety, good soil.

The years of self-righteousness from my perceived lack of visible sin, good soil.

The years involved in serving in ministries, good soil.

Yet finally, here I am—the closest to Jesus I've ever been, the wisest I've ever been, the most content I've ever been—and I can finally see the real soil I've been.

Let me be transparent with you, it's not the good soil.

I've spent most of my life as *the path*—as soon as something good happened, my anxiety disorder would convince me otherwise. Any hope and joy I found was fleeting, gone in an instant—just as the birds picked the seed from the path.

Then, there were countless years I spent as the *rocky soil*.

I remember during my college years when I found Christianity and met a different form of Jesus than I had been brought up believing in the Catholic Church. This Jesus was more real and more relatable, and I loved him—on Sundays.

However, once the week came back around and fraternity nightlife began, the obedience-to and confidence-in Jesus was thrown on the back-burner. I had multiple lords over my life for six days of the week.

I wasn't going to be the only person at the party who wasn't indulging. Do you want to stick out like a sore thumb? I was not about to be made fun of and outcast from my group.

I can't fail to mention a memory: a fellow fraternity member took the podium at one of our meetings and explained he had found Christ and was leaving due to what the fraternity lifestyle entailed and how it didn't coincide with the life Christ calls us to. I now see that as a bold, courageous, and strong action but viewed it through a much different lens at the time.

What a loser! What a Jesus freak!

We made fun of him on his way out of the door, but I have not forgotten the moment.

As for the last few years, I believe I've lived a life resembling the seed amongst thorns. When I became a Christian at 24-years old, I finally began to experience sobriety from alcohol and drug use, as well as healing from my anxiety disorder. For the first time in my life I was no longer afraid to announce my faith—instead I was proud of it. Joy and hope were found in me for the first time in as long as I could remember. I found community and vulnerability and intentionality, and my life experienced this overflow of freedom I never thought would happen for me. It started a season of such dramatic transformation in my life.

Then, however, I realized the way God was asking me to date wasn't the way I wanted to date. Then, the dreams I sought appeared different than what God had planned for me. Then, God asked me to give up things I didn't want to give up—and he asked me to carry things I didn't want to carry. He asked me to share things I didn't want to share, and to walk through things I had long buried. He asked me to be still and patient when I was ready to move and move quickly.

I struggled mightily to overcome my desire to quit trying to change and to revert back to how I had lived before Christ.

My point is this—it was different from what I expected.

Much different.

The joy I thought I would find in things he gave me, was instead meant to be found in what he had already done for me. The hope I sought was rooted in a hope that he would grant my desires in this life. Instead, as I have later come to understand, the hope He gives is hope for the next life and hope that he alone is enough to sustain me in this life.

I think the Pharisees ran into a similar problem when Jesus came but wasn't what they expected. He came to show them what truly good soil looked like. He came to show them *"the way, and the truth, and the life"*[3] but it was much different than what they envisioned.

Instead of a Messiah coming to save Israel from Rome, Jesus spent more time focused on saving poor people from religious leaders. Instead of a Messiah coming to unite the various sects of followers under the One True God of Israel, Jesus came and told the religious leaders they were going to hell if they didn't repent. Instead of a Messiah establishing an earthly kingdom with domain over everyone, Jesus came to wash feet and save prostitutes and lepers. Instead of the prophesied all-powerful Messiah, Jesus was born in a manger next to livestock and raised in humble Galilee.[4]

Jesus didn't fit the picture of what was expected. In fact, he wasn't even close. He was, at the same time, both much less and much greater than

---

3. John 14:6

4. John 7:52 says, "They replied, "Are you from Galilee, too? Look into it, and you will find that a prophet does not come out of Galilee.""

imaginable. He didn't live in a palace or control the most powerful army on earth. He didn't even have a comfortable spot to lay his head.[5] He didn't have any money and he wasn't even pleasant to look at.[6]

Yet the areas in which He is greater-than are infinitely more than where he was less. He came to do what no one else could ever do. He loved those who the world rejected, and he loved those who hated him. He showed the world what love was when the world had no idea. He died so you and I could have his spirit and spend eternity with him.

The grace of it all is unbelievable. Again, this is nowhere near the correct word, but I suppose there is no word great enough to explain what Jesus did for us.

Now, I can look back and finally distinguish that all the time I thought I was good soil, I was actually everything but.

Today, after 10,051 days of believing I've been the good soil, I realize what I've truly been—my life has been a hodgepodge of concrete and rocky soil, of thorn-covered brush, and of shallow soil.

Which means today starts another countdown.

Today is Day One of my life where I recognize I'm everything but the good soil. And it's my hope that my awareness of this fact will keep me from allowing *"the worries of this life, the deceitfulness of wealth and the desires for other things [to] come in and choke the word, making it unfruitful."*[7]

Who knows? Maybe one day I'll be able to look back and see that the first day I saw myself as something other than the good soil, was really my first day as the good soil.

I hope and have prayed for you, reader—that today or tomorrow or the next day may be your first day as good soil. I've hoped and prayed you should come to understand and know Jesus by first identifying with those who missed him; by identifying with those who dedicated their entire lives to serving and praising God and missed him as he stood next to them—that you may be humble enough to accept that you probably aren't smarter than them, or more dedicated, or sacrificed more, or that you're in any way different.

5. Luke 9:58 says, "Jesus replied, "Foxes have dens and birds have nests, but the Son of Man has no place to lay his head."

6. In Isaiah 52:14, the prophet Isaiah prophesies about Jesus. "Just as there were many who were appalled at him—his appearance was so disfigured beyond that of any human being and his form marred beyond human likeness."

7. Mark 4:19

It's my hope and prayer that in fact what makes you different from them is that you believe yourself to be one of them—a hypocrite, a sinner, unworthy, and dishonorable, with nothing to offer God.

In the same way that God is never changing and always perfect, we as humans are always the same, except sinful. We are wrong and will always be wrong, just as Paul explains in Romans chapter 7:

> "We know that the law is spiritual; but I am unspiritual, sold as a slave to sin. [15]I do not understand what I do. For what I want to do I do not do, but what I hate I do. [16]And if I do what I do not want to do, I agree that the law is good. [17]As it is, it is no longer I myself who do it, but it is sin living in me. [18]For I know that good itself does not dwell in me, that is, in my sinful nature. For I have the desire to do what is good, but I cannot carry it out. [19]For I do not do the good I want to do, but the evil I do not want to do—this I keep on doing. [20]Now if I do what I do not want to do, it is no longer I who do it, but it is sin living in me that does it.
>
> [21]So I find this law at work: Although I want to do good, evil is right there with me. [22]For in my inner being I delight in God's law; [23]but I see another law at work in me, waging war against the law of my mind and making me a prisoner of the law of sin at work within me. [24]What a wretched man I am! Who will rescue me from this body that is subject to death? [25]Thanks be to God, who delivers me through Jesus Christ our Lord!"[8]

∼ ∾

It's my prayer and hope that this book has taken you on a journey of your own, in a similar manner to the one it's given me. When you turn the final page of this book, instead of feeling compelled to *do something*, you're convicted to *be someone*—to be someone who may recognize Jesus today when everyone else misses him. To be someone who serves instead of symbolizing serving. To be someone who is willing to lay down their life when the Spirit asks them to.

If, after all this, you're still searching for where to start—at what the next tangible step may look like—then I recommend this:

---

8. Romans 7:14–25

Take a deep breath.
Forget everything you think you know.
Turn back to the prologue.
Repeat the following: Woe to You, Me.
And start again.

"For the kingdom of heaven is like a landowner who went out early in the morning to hire workers for his vineyard. He agreed to pay them a denarius for the day and sent them into his vineyard.

About nine in the morning he went out and saw others standing in the marketplace doing nothing. He told them, 'You also go and work in my vineyard, and I will pay you whatever is right.' So they went.

He went out again about noon and about three in the afternoon and did the same thing. About five in the afternoon he went out and found still others standing around. He asked them, 'Why have you been standing here all day long doing nothing?'

'Because no one has hired us,' they answered.

He said to them, 'You also go and work in my vineyard.'

When evening came, the owner of the vineyard said to his foreman, 'Call the workers and pay them their wages, beginning with the last ones hired and going on to the first.'

The workers who were hired about five in the afternoon came and each received a denarius. So when those came who were hired first, they expected to receive more. But each one of them also received a denarius. When they received it, they began to grumble against the landowner. 'There who were hired last worked only one hour,' they said, 'and you have made them equal to us who have borne the burden of the work and the heat of the day.'

But he answered one of them, 'I am not being unfair to you, friend. Didn't you agree to work for a denarius? Take your pay and go. I want to give the one who was hired last the same as I gave you. Don't I have the right to do what I want with my own money? Or are you envious because I am generous?'

So the last will be first, and the first will be last."

MATTHEW 20:1–16

Bibliography

"50 Most Popular & Favorite Bible Verses—Top Read Scripture Quotes." Bible Study Tools. Salem Web Network, 2020. https://www.biblestudytools.com/topical-verses/the-25-most-read-bible-verses/.

"Ancient Jewish History: Pharisees, Sadducees & Essenes." Accessed 2019. Jewish Virtual Library, https://www.jewishvirtuallibrary.org/pharisees-sadducees-and-essenes.

Budge, Earnest Alfred Thompson Wallis. *The Book of the Bee*. Oxford: Clarendon, 1886.

Casson, Lionel. *Travel in the Ancient World*. Rev. ed. Baltimore, MD: Johns Hopkins University Press, 1974.

"Christians Are the Largest Religious Group in 2015." Pew Research Center, April 4, 2017. https://www.pewresearch.org/fact-tank/2017/04/05/christians-remain-worlds-largest-religious-group-but-they-are-declining-in-europe/ft_17-14-05_projectionsupdate_globalpop640px/.

Cunningham, John M. "Pharisee." Encyclopædia Britannica, May 5, 2014. https://www.britannica.com/topic/Pharisee.

David, Jonathan, and Melissa Helser. "The Kind of Worship God Desires." *Jonathan David and Melissa Helser Podcast*. Lecture presented at the Jonathan David and Melissa Helser Podcast, April 14, 2020.

Duffin, Jacalyn. "Sweating Blood: History and Review." *Canadian Medical Association Journal* 189, no. 42 (October 23, 2017) E1315-E1317. https://doi.org/10.1503/cmaj.170756.

Epstein, Joseph. "Think You Have a Book in You? Think Again." *The New York Times*, September 28, 2002.

Garroway, Joshua. "Pharisees." Bible Odyssey. Accessed April 23, 2020. https://www.bibleodyssey.org/en/people/main-articles/pharisees.

Gill, John. *John Gill's Exposition of the Bible*. Exposition of the Old and New Testament, 1746. https://www.biblestudytools.com/commentaries/gills-exposition-of-the-bible/.

Huckey, Darren. "Whitewashed Tombs." *Emet Hatorah* (blog). Accessed April 29, 2020. https://www.emethatorah.com/blog/2016/october-10/whitewashed-tombs.

"Jewish Practices & Rituals." Mikveh. Accessed April 29, 2020. https://www.jewishvirtuallibrary.org/mikveh.

Lamm, Maurice. "The Jewish Marriage Contract (Ketubah)." Chabad.Org, June 26, 2007. https://www.chabad.org/library/article_cdo/aid/465168/jewish/The-Jewish-Marriage-Contract-Ketubah.htm.

"Leaning Tower of Pisa." Leaning Tower of Pisa, 2018. http://www.towerofpisa.org/leaning-tower-of-pisa-history/.

Lexico Dictionaries | English. Lexico Dictionaries by Oxford. Accessed April 22, 2020. https://www.lexico.com (Pharisee, Pride, and Insolent).

Life Application Study Bible. Grand Rapids, MI: Zondervan, 2011.

"Local Mediterranean Winds." Mediterranean Sailing, Cruising, Navigation. Mediterranean Winds., 2010. http://www.1yachtua.com/Medit-marinas/Mediterranean_Sailing/mediterranean_winds.shtm.

Mackie, George M. *Bible Manners and Customs*. New York: Fleming H. Revell, 1898.

Merenlahti, Petri. "Judaism in the Time of Jesus." Judaism in the Time of Jesus. University of Helsinki. Accessed April 22, 2020. http://www.helsinki.fi/teol/pro/_merenlah/oppimateriaalit/text/english/judaism.htm.

O'Reilly, Bill, and Martin Dugard. *Killing Jesus: A History*. New York: St Martin's Press, 2018.

"Passover in Israel—Past and Present." Chosen People Ministries, March 17, 2020. https://www.chosenpeople.com/site/passover-in-israel-past-and-present/.

Piper, John. "John the Baptist and the Brood of Vipers." *Desiring God*, February 9, 1981. https://www.desiringgod.org/messages/john-the-baptist-and-the-brood-of-vipers.

Poole, Matthew. *A Commentary on the Holy Bible: v. 3. Matthew to Revelation*. Edinburgh: Banner of Truth Trust, 1963.

Rodkinson, Michael Levi, et al. *New Edition of the Babylonian Talmud*. New York: Talmud Society, 1918.

"Sadducees." Livius, 1996. https://www.livius.org/articles/people/sadducees/.

Schauss, Hayyim. "Ancient Jewish Marriage." My Jewish Learning. Accessed April 28, 2020. https://www.myjewishlearning.com/article/ancient-jewish-marriage/.

"Sepphoris." Livius, 2017. https://www.livius.org/articles/place/sepphoris/.

Skinner, Betty Lee. *Daws: The Story of Dawson Trotman*. Grand Rapids, MI: Zondervan, 1974.

Slattery, Jennifer. "10 Common Idols in Our Lives and How to Resist Them." Bible Study Tools, 2019.

Todd, Michael. "Bandwagon Believer." *Who's The Minister Here?* Sermon presented at Transformation Church, Tusla, OK, April 19, 2020.

Wellhausen, Julius, and Mark Edward Biddle. *The Pharisees and the Sadducees: an Examination of Internal Jewish History*. Macon, GA: Mercer University Press, 2001.

Wight, Fred H. *Manners and Customs of Bible Lands*. Chicago: Moody, 1983.

"You Might Be An Idolater If . . ." Crossway, October 21, 2014. https://www.crossway.org/articles/you-might-be-an-idolater-if/.

www.ingramcontent.com/pod-product-compliance
Lightning Source LLC
Chambersburg PA
CBHW060341100426
42812CB00003B/1084